Planning, Scheduling

and

Requirement Analysis

First Edition

Connie Hinson, CPPO, CPPB
and
Clifford P. McCue, Ph.D.
Associate Professor
School of Public Administration
Florida Atlantic University

Prepared for the National Institute of Governmental Purchasing under the LEAP
Program. All rights are conveyed to the NIGP upon completion of this book.

Planning, Scheduling and Requirement Analysis

ISBN number 1-932315-02-0

This book was set in Berkeley Oldstyle
Design and layout by Vizuäl, Inc.
Printing by HBP.

LE P
Learning and Education to Advance Procurement

The National Institute of Governmental Purchasing gratefully acknowledges financial contributions from the following organizations.

Patron Sponsors

Office Depot

IAPSO

Gold Level Friends

Florida Association of Public Purchasing Officers, Inc.

LES Professional Development Foundation

Virginia Association of Governmental Purchasing Chapter of NIGP, Inc.

Silver Level Friends

CDW Corporation

Georgia Chapter of NIGP

Louisiana Chapter of NIGP

Southeast Florida Chapter of NIGP

Bronze Level Friends

Columbia Chapter of NIGP

Mr. Steven H. Corwin, CPPO, C.P.M.

Governmental Purchasing Association of Georgia Chapter of NIGP

Gulf Coast Association of Governmental Purchasing Officers, Inc.
Chapter of NIGP

Kentucky Public Procurement Association Chapter of NIGP

New York State Association of Municipal Purchasing Officials
Chapter of NIGP

Ontario Public Buyers Association, Inc. Chapter of NIGP

San Antonio Public Purchasing Association Chapter of NIGP

Southeast Louisiana Chapter of NIGP

Southeast Texas Association of Public Purchasing Chapter of NIGP

Tampa Bay Area Chapter of NIGP

Wisconsin Association of Public Purchasers Chapter of NIGP

The contributions listed above were received and recorded as of **June 15, 2004.**

Patron Level - $50,000 • Gold Level Friends - $10,000 - 19,999

Silver Level Friends - $5,000 - $9,999 • Bronze Level Friends - $1,000 - 4,999

WITH APPRECIATION

Procurement professionals have historically risen through the ranks of government employment with little or no formal education in their chosen profession. Out of this awareness, the idea behind the LEAP program was conceived. In the fall of 2000, the program was first presented to the Board of Directors of the National Institute of Governmental Purchasing (NIGP) and given a vote of confidence to continue. From that time on, work has not ceased to make this vision become reality. With a mission to build a new educational framework that provides the procurement professional with knowledge and the potential for more rigorous formalized educational opportunities supported by academia, this project is just the beginning of what we perceive to be the commencement of public procurement education reform.

We cannot do justice to the many people who have been a part of the formidable effort required in the writing and production of these books. We would be remiss however, if we did not acknowledge the staff of NIGP, who contributed countless hours of work to the project with commitment and dedication. Donna Beach, CPPO, CPPB, C.P.M., Rick Grimm, CPPO, CPPB, Carol Hodes, and Sandy Riggs have offered insights, editorial comments, revision expertise and emotional and physical support to all involved. A special thanks to Roylene Sims, the copy editor, and Bill Hertwig, CPPO, CPPB, C.P.M., A.P.P., who spent numerous hours reading the text to ensure quality, credibility and consistency throughout. Members, NIGP instructors and committed professionals, too numerous to mention here, volunteered their time to read countless drafts and offer suggestions to the authors as the work began to take form.

This project is dedicated to the men and women who serve the public by striving to make quality public procurement decisions. Such commitment to excellence will undoubtedly change the face of public procurement in academia and in the workplace.

DEDICATION

*T*his book is dedicated to our families, Jacki, Jordon, and Ryan McCue and Dick Hinson. Without their support, both intellectually and pragmatically, and without their willingness to endure many hours of lost family time, this book would not have been possible. It is their book as much as it is ours. This book is also dedicated to our professional colleagues in the procurement "trenches." We hope the book serves as a vehicle to aid in developing the field and provides useful information that can be used to better their stations in life. Keep the faith!

ACKNOWLEDGMENTS

All authors must be aware of their dependence on the extant literature and the accumulated knowledge of their subject fields, particularly when writing textbooks. We are much indebted to a great many who have published their concepts and findings—both in scholarly journals and professional publications. They are identified largely in the footnotes citing their works. Unfortunately, the extant literature in public sector procurement is particularly arid, so many cites are from private sector sources.

Some fellow academicians have more directly contributed with suggestions and stimulating ideas at various Learning and Education to Advance Procurement (LEAP) symposiums over the last two years, among whom are Drs. Jerry Gianakis, Larry Martin, Jack Pitzer, Wendell Lawther, Carol Pettijohn, Linda Stanley, Khi Thai, Charles Washington, and Elisabeth Wright. Some fellow practicing procurement professionals who also greatly added to the development of this book at the LEAP symposium are John Adler, CPPO; Ken Babich, CPPO, B.COM; Kirk Buffington, C.P.M.; Bill Davison, CPPO; Tony Ellis, CPPO; Michael Flynn, Esq.; Darin Matthews, CPPO, C.P.M.; and John Miller, CPPO. In addition, we must personally thank each author of previous editions of the *General Public Procurement* text. Their work, and attribution in Chapters 2, 3, and 4, is greatly appreciated.

From the professional world, we have enjoyed the assistance of a number of individuals who are engaged in procurement and procurement planning. They probably cannot all be recalled, as the creation of this book extended over a number of years. Specifically, we would like to note the contributions of Al Bettencourt, CPPO, CPPB; Bill Brady, CPPO; Cindy Dahl, CPPB, C.P.M.; Wendy Geltch, CPPO, CPPB, C.P.M.; Keith Glatz, CPPO, Bobbie Ogletree, CPPO; and Melinda Via, CPPO. In particular, a special thanks goes to the Queensland State Government, Department of Public Works, Queensland Purchasing Division (Christine Tonkin, Director) for allowing us to use their conceptual model of procurement planning presented in Chapter 3. Not only do they provide cutting edge information on procurement planning, they also understand the critical link between organizational strategic planning and procurement planning. Cheers to our Queensland colleagues.

The support furnished by the National Institute of Governmental Purchasing (NIGP) through the LEAP program and the Public Procurement Research Center (PPRC) at Florida Atlantic University must be described as ideal, particularly on the part of Rick Grimm, CPPO, CPPB, Carol Hodes and Natalie

Pulsifer from the NIGP, and Dr. Khi Thai with the PPRC. Remarkably thorough and intelligent copy editing by Roylene Sims has greatly improved the manuscript. Notable improvements can also be attributed to the number of individuals who participated in various NIGP Forum events to help flush-out the contents and nature of the book. Particularly among our many professional colleagues, we would like to recognize Dick Florey, CPPO, and Elene Fromanger, CPPO, CPPB, for their patience (and critique) in reading various drafts of this book. Their insights and continued support of this effort were untiring and greatly appreciated.

The book's virtues are partially attributable to the above, but any faults or errors belong purely to us. We will be grateful to the readers who inform us about the latter.

CONTENTS

PREFACE

In Planning, Scheduling and Requirement Analysis, we have sought to write a textbook that will inform and attract a reader by its clear statement of principles and methods, realism, and its engagement of the reader through intellectual expansion and critique. We trust that both current procurement professionals and academics will find it quite tenable and that its illustrations, figures, and discussion of key points are both enlightening and engaging. More importantly, we hope that both practitioners and academics find the material essential to the procurement function and critical to the development of the field.

In the private sector, trends in corporate restructuring have focused on project-oriented or product-oriented production and sales processes, which have resulted in flatter, more horizontal organizational structures (Freeman & Cavinata, 1990; Morrison, 1997; Garrent, 1996). Much of the drive towards global restructuring is increased productivity and higher quality, where procurement is seen as a key ingredient to enhancing a firm's competitive advantage (Rajagopal & Bernard, 1993; Heberling, 1993; Ruacco & Proctor, 1994). Public sector organizations have, to a much lesser degree, been impacted by these changes. Under the auspices of the "Reinventing Government" movement (Gore, 1993), governments continue to face pressures to decouple organizational structures, deregulate policies and procedures, empower service delivery managers, and embrace client needs; where economy and efficiency are the primary concerns of decision-makers and consumers alike (Frayer & Monezka, 1997). These pressures have been particularly felt in the procurement arena, where service delivery managers, elected officials, and customers are calling for procurement reform (McCue & Pitzer, 2000).

The progress of public sector organizations since the 1980s has generated increased demand for procurement planning, scheduling, and requirement analysis and participation by procurement professionals in the actual implementation of many restructuring projects—particularly out-sourcing and privatization (Humphreys, McIvor & McAleer, 1998). The increased demand for procurement's participation in organizational decision making and participation in resource allocation decisions has not been met by an increased contribution to the organization's strategic mission by procurement professionals. This limitation is most noteworthy in service delivery areas where procurement can play a vital consultancy role, such as capital planning and budgeting, or where the use of external consultants makes good economic sense, such as architectural and engineering services, but entré into the organization is limited.

By enhancing the strategic position of procurement and by advancing the analytical capacities of procurement professionals, the procurement profession can become a more powerful instrument within public organizations. Procurement can provide a high-quality, across-the-board, integrative mechanism to modernize public sector strategic efforts around the main goals and objectives of improving service development and delivery systems. In addition to their strategic capabilities, procurement professionals, for example, should be actively involved in tactical projects, such as process restructuring projects; evaluating the cost effectiveness of privatization and out-sourcing; assisting in the development of quality management/quality assurance systems; and actively participating in evaluating productivity enhancements for most service delivery options.

All of these considerations, together with the lack of available information and publications and the growing demand for more information on procurement planning, scheduling, and requirement analysis has prompted us to produce this book. The main target groups of the book are:

- Public sector procurement professionals;
- State and local governments' service delivery managers;
- Line and staff personnel representing present and/or future procurement stakeholders;
- The supplier/vendor community;
- Elected officials;
- Management training and development professionals; and
- Management practitioners, students and training program participants interested in expanding their understanding of the various methods and approaches to strategic planning, process restructuring and increased organizational performance.

In addition to the groups identified above, the text is written primarily as an introduction to the strategic planning/procurement planning process for students of public procurement. Although emphasis is placed on the procurement practitioner, the ultimate audience for the text is current and future procurement professionals attempting to advance the field and develop their knowledge, skills and abilities relative to procurement's strategic position in an organization. In light of the broad nature of an introductory text, many of the concepts may be familiar to the practicing public administrator and public procurement professionals. However, for the vast majority of individuals interested in learning more about the relationship between strategic planning, procurement planning, requirement analysis and selection, this book will greatly add to their toolbox of skills and abilities to advance the profession.

Chapter 1 discusses the changing role of procurement and the need for its involvement in the resource allocation and strategic planning processes. The discussion is based upon a conceptual model used for strategic planning that characterizes procurement as a discipline and develops procurement theory to describe the profession. The legitimacy of the model rests on the assumption that procurement is a central "player" in the resource allocation process within public organizations and that procurement planning and strategic planning is interconnected. The roles of procurement (service, staff and line) and where procurement reports within the organization are examined from the more traditional approach that focuses on current operational service to expanding staff and line roles to increase functional authority and greater involvement in the strategic planning process.

Chapter 2 examines strategic planning in the public sector, including the expansion of the conceptual model introduced in Chapter 1. The model posits that strategic planning is a set of concepts, techniques and tools that help an organization assess where it is, decide where it wants to go and determine the best way to get there. In order to effectuate this simple process, procurement professionals must become actively involved in the development and implementation of strategic plans.

The relationship of strategic planning to procurement planning is discussed in Chapter 3. The purpose of this chapter is to provide procurement professionals with the basic knowledge and techniques of planning and to show readers how to transform the organizational mission, goals and objectives into measurable activities to be used to plan, budget and manage the procurement function. At the conclusion of the chapter, professionals should know how to develop a strategic procurement plan as a management tool that reinforces the strategic plan of the organization and enhances procurement's role in allocation decisions.

The relationship between planning and resource allocation is a critical dimension of strategic planning success. Therefore, the budget process, budget types and budget models are detailed in Chapter 4. Procurement should have a strategic role in the budget process but has historically been left out of this critical function. As previously noted, this omission of procurement from resource allocation results in fragmentation and little value to the organization.

Chapter 5 discusses procurement strategies in relation to requirements determination. Again, the need for procurement to be involved in the budget process is emphasized, particularly how the planning process is negatively impacted when it does not participate. Defining customer needs, researching previous purchases based upon procurement analysis techniques, assessing market conditions and determining the method of solicitation are examined as mechanisms to achieve value.

Specifications are examined in Chapter 6. The types of specifications and appropriate use are probably already familiar to the student. We maintain that specification development follows and should build upon requirements determination in order to avoid the potential problem of the "cart before the horse" syndrome.

Chapter 7 analyzes pricing strategies and how they can be used effectively in the strategic planning and requirements determination processes. When evaluation techniques, such as life-cycle costing, price analysis and cost analysis, are used effectively, they result in additional value to the organization produced by the procurement agency. Often, this link is not recognized as a substantive part of the procurement process—adding value to the organization—but, in Chapter 7, it is professed that this critical link is necessary to further advance the field and locate procurement as a value-adding enterprise in the organization.

Chapter 8 summarizes the role and importance of strategic planning to the procurement process and offers a synthesis of the topics covered in this book. The emphasis of this chapter is to challenge the academics who teach procurement and the many individuals who practice procurement to think about procurement planning, scheduling, and requirement analysis as a necessary ingredient in the efficient and effective allocation of public resources and, ultimately, how procurement can impact the health and vitality of the communities in which they reside.

References

Frayer, D. J., & Monczka, R. M. (1997). Enhanced strategic competitiveness through global supply chain management. *Annual Conference of the Council of Logistics Management*, 433-441.

Freeman, V., & Cavinato, J. (1990). Fitting purchasing to the strategic firm: frameworks, processes, and values. *Journal of Purchasing and Materials Management*, 26(1), 19-25.

Garrent, B. (1996). *Strategic thinking: Developing strategic thought.* New York: Harper-Collins Publishing.

Gore, A. (1993). *Creating a government that works better and costs less: Report of the National Performance Review.* Washington, DC: U.S. Government Printing Office.

Heberling, M. E. (1993). The rediscovery of modern purchasing. *International Journal of Purchasing and Materials Management*, 29(4), 48-53.

Humphreys, P., McIvor, P., & McAleer, E. (1998). The purchasing function as a professional service firm: Implications for training and development. *Journal of European Industrial Training*, 22(1), 3-11.

McCue, C. P., & Pitzer, J. T. (2000). Centralized vs. decentralized purchasing: Current trends in governmental procurement practices. *Journal of Public Budgeting, Accounting & Financial Management*, 12(3), 400-420.

Morrison, I. (1997). *Second curve: Managing the velocity of change.* London: Nicholas Brealey Publishing.

Rajagopal, S., & Bernard, K. (1993). Strategic procurement and competitive advantage. *Journal of Purchasing and Material Management*, 13-20.

Ruocco, P., & Proctor, T. (1994). Strategic planning in practice: A creative approach. *Marketing Intelligence & Planning*, 12(9), 24-29.

CHAPTER 1

Strategy and Choice:
Procurement's Involvement in Organizational Decision Making

*T*he purchasing function has undergone significant change over the last two decades, where a "new" view of procurement has emerged (Humphrey, McIvor & McAleer 1998; MacBeth & Ferguson 1994). Facing rising input costs, rapidly changing technology, global competition, product complexity, corporate downsizing, and increasing customer demands, a significant number of firms have realized the advantage of optimizing the organizational value-chain (Ferguson et al, 1996; Gadde, & Hakansson, 1994). Through strategic alliance of procurement in corporate decision making, a number of firms have realized the increased benefits of procurement's involvement in expanding market share/profits through cost reduction/cost avoidance, customer service, continuity of supply, and input quality (Thompson, 1996; Whaetley, 1998; Spekmam, Kamauff, & Salmond, 1994; Saunders, 1994). What these organizations have found is that procurement is just as critical in maintaining their competitive advantage as other more traditional functions, such as finance, production and, even, marketing (Watts, Kim, & Hahn, 1992). Consequently, the roles and responsibilities of procurement have significantly broadened within private organizations, and a number of firms have elevated procurement to a strategic corporate position.

Like their private sector counterparts, turbulence in the operating environment of public sector organizations, primarily stemming from rapidly emerging technologies, product diversification, environmental issues, and the increased emphasis on quality and best value (not simply lowest price) has made the public sector procurement just as complex (Bryson, 1995; Quayle & Quayle, 2000). Today, public sector procurement professionals face social, political, and economic values that attempt to satisfy the requirements of fairness, equity, and transparency, while maximizing competition and increasing economy and efficiency (Koteen, 1989; McCue & Gianakis 2001). Within these often competing and conflicting demands, procurement organizations confront declining resources, higher demands for flexibility and operational responsiveness, and limited strategic support within the organization (Quayle & Quayle, 2000; McCue & Pitzer, 2000).

Adding to the complexity of public sector procurement, purchasing has been spotlighted by a number of academics and public officials as a target for reform. Efforts to engage and empower service delivery managers to meet the needs of citizens by granting them greater flexibility in the use of public resources in exchange for holding them accountable for the achievement of service objectives is resonant in contemporary governance (Osborne & Gaebler, 1992; Osborne & Plastrik, 1997). According to Gianakis and McCue (1999), public sector service delivery managers are held accountable for the efficient discharge of public resources through controls on their use of inputs into the service production/delivery process. This control is exercised through political and administrative mechanisms, traditionally through centralized command structures that are often referred to as bureaucratic obstacles. Reformers contend that controls on the factors of production constrain the ability of service managers to meet service demands efficiently and effectively. Deregulating purchasing control and decentralizing (decoupling) the purchasing function is beginning to receive modest attention in government (Gianakis & Wang, 2000; McCue & Pitzer, 2000).

Despite the increased turbulence in the procurement environment and the increasing calls for procurement reform, the procurement function in the public sector has not reached the same status as its private sector counterparts. Nor has the public sector procurement function received a great deal of academic attention from public administration scholars (Thai, 2001; MacManus, 1992). Currently, many state and local governments are considering alternative delivery systems, such as outsourcing, to reduce costs and increase efficiency in public sector purchasing (i.e., "reinvent" purchasing processes). This involves searching for ways of streamlining the entire supply-chain/value-chain process—the ordering of goods and services, warehousing and inventory decisions, and electronic purchasing. Thai (2001, p. 64) contends that structural/technological change will, in turn, shift the way public procurement systems are viewed; specifically, decisions affecting the management of public organizations, such as make or buy decisions, decentralization of procurement decision-making, and deregulation of control systems.

There are a host of reasons why procurement research has received limited academic and practical attention, most noticeably in linking strategic planning and procurement planning. One reason that little attention has been given to the relative importance of procurement in the strategic planning process can be attributed to the fact that procurement professionals are not typically viewed as strategic partners in the development and delivery of public goods and services. Purchasing, after all, is perceived as a service function relegated to "clerical staff" that are commonly seen as institutional gatekeepers and bureaucratic obstacles that inhibit the effective management of organizational resources (Gore, 1993; Wildavsky, 1984). Even when change agents are developed in the market, such as electronic purchasing, these individuals inhibit change and promote rule-driven bureaucratic structures.

Another reason for the lack of strategic importance of procurement could be attributable to the procurement profession itself. This is most problematic, given the fact that a significant number of purchasing agents have failed to enhance their knowledge, skills, and abilities within the public management spectrum (NIGP 2000). Other reasons could include the fact that there has been limited theorizing about the nature of the public procurement process and how the field of public procurement plays a critical role in the resource allocation process of governments. Currently, as a result of the limited normative or descriptive theoretical development of public procurement, procurement has no legitimacy as an independent field of study or as a strategic partner in allocating organizational resources.

This chapter attempts to delineate a conceptual model of public procurement that can enhance the strategic importance of the procurement profession. The model offered in this text characterizes procurement generally as a central partner in the resource allocation process of public organizations—organizations that continually operate in highly competitive and disperse political environments and whose boundaries are shaped in large part through statutory requirements, operational norms, institutional arrangements, managerial beliefs, and procurement transparency (Gianakis & McCue, 1999). The model reflects the assumption that as a strategic partner in allocating organizational resources, public procurement scholars and professionals should attempt to develop normative and descriptive theories that are relevant for both public procurement professionals and service delivery managers. Such integrative theories and techniques should identify possibilities for, and limitations to, action or, at a minimum, illuminate the nature of the strategic environment of public procurement in the context of optimizing the resource allocation process of government.

If students and practitioners view the procurement process from the perspective of managers charged with the development and delivery of public goods and services and, ultimately, the impact that procurement has on the consumers of public goods and services, procurement theory can begin to establish itself as a self-identified discipline. Like any other manager, procurement professionals practice in the structure, culture, processes, and procedures of the public organization; and its network of environmental relationships define the action environment by which they respond. To dismiss these dimensions in the development of procurement theory will continue to lead to describing how they currently manage without reference to how things ought to be. This normative perspective provides glimpses of future procurement practices and will allow the field to develop and nourish (Gianakis & McCue, 1999; McCue & Gianakis, 2001; Thai, 2001).

The second assumption reflected in this model is that procurement is a multi-disciplinary field that should attempt to define itself as a value-adding discipline. By continuing to focus on purchasing as a service function, procurement will continue to duplicate theories and concepts developed elsewhere. Like other fields that draw upon other disciplines, such as business administration, public procurement is constrained by the organizational structures and processes (both institutional and programmatic) inherent in the delivery of societal goods and services, given the community's preferences for governance structures and political processes (Gianakis & McCue, 1999). The responsibility to optimize the relationship between operational technologies and organizational structures (the resource allocation process) and for managing the operational activities of complex organizations suggests that the procurement profession needs to borrow from a variety of substantive areas. The focus on the integrative nature of public procurement justifies these borrowings, and the development of procurement theory must be examined in the context of its strategic importance to organizational effectiveness.

The third assumption is that procurement professionals must examine their behaviors relative to their impact on the development and delivery of public services. All too often we dismiss the actions of these individuals, assuming them to be emotion-free individuals acting in the rational interests of the organization. Given a procurement decision point, procurement professionals act in the best interests of the organization. This assumption is limited. A considerable amount of research has been conducted on the rational behavior of managers, although the procurement manager's behavior is not studied extensively. In general, research suggests that most decision sequences apply a modified rational process (Wildavsky, 1984). In very complex decisions, such as a large construction project, the decision sequence tends to include both emotional and rational dimensions (Taylor & Hussey, 1982; Wildavsky, 1984). The behavior of procurement professionals, such as risk-taking characteristics, should be examined, when looking at the impact procurement has on the allocation process of governments.

Ultimately, the legitimacy of the model rests on the assumption that procurement is a central component of the resource allocation process within public organizations. In this light, public procurement is viewed from the totality of the processes and products of public service delivery systems and the underlying support structures, not simply from functional "silos" that have traditionally characterized government hierarchal structures. The variety of service delivery systems that comprises the organization and the necessary deference that must be paid to substantive expertise in various organizational processes, such as human resource management, finance, and procurement, suggests that public organizations are highly differentiated and very complex systems—so much so that the concept of a single integrated organization can be elusive, particularly at the federal level, where cross-functional systems break down completely (Wildavsky, 1984; Gianakis & McCue, 1999).

Like most organizations, the federal government is an enterprise that is comprised of a variety of sub-enterprises, each of which enjoys a relative degree of autonomy from the authority of the chief executive. From a conceptual standpoint, these agencies can be perceived as semi-independent agencies rather than as elements of a single integrated organization (MacManus, 1992). State and local governments are also highly differentiated. Individual agencies respond to particular consumer demands and employ different perspectives in what is a highly decentralized policy-making environment. In turn, the weakly integrated organization is highly permeable to the political environment and is subject to enormous forces by a strong chief executive (Gianakis & McCue, 1999). From a rational perspective, these forces inevitably constrain the allocative efficiency of the resource allocation process. In loosely coupled systems (where there is no central integration), the resource allocation process can become purely a function of political power and in-fighting rather than the product of institutional planning regarding the actual needs of the jurisdiction. In short, the resource allocation process is skewed towards those agencies that can muster the strongest political support.

The emphasis on an integrated organization under the rubric of strategic planning does not mean that the framework provided in this book simply calls for moving the foci of procurement research from the examination of the institutional arrangements and the tools and techniques used in the procurement processes, which some have contended may be fertile ground for procurement theory building (Glueck & Jauch, 1984; McCue & Gianakis, 2000; Schreyog & Steinmann, 1987; Thai, 2001). The model posited in this text suggests that the procurement planning process and the strategic planning process are interconnected; and, in order to effectuate either, both must be present. Neither the formal strategic planning process nor the operational planning process captures the continuous nature of the procurement process—a characteristic that is only just beginning to be recognized by academic theorists. The procurement process of the public organization is characterized by a continuous series of disaggregated, overlapping, and fragmented, but nevertheless interdependent, parallel decision sequences (Haines, 2000). In most cases, these decision sequences lack a strategic perspective. It is at this point that the allocation process resembles a disjointed set of decision sequences. By examining procurement as an integrative mechanism (coupling the organization through the procurement process), the roots of synthesis can grow.

...procurement planning process and the strategic planning process are interconnected...

The salient dimensions of the procurement process are described in more detail in the next section. The extent to which public procurement may differ from private sector procurement and, hence, may require different approaches to theory development is also briefly explored. This is followed by a re-conceptualization of the public procurement process as a strategic component in the resource allocation process of governments, identifying the critical dimensions necessary to accomplish both the strategic mission of the organization and the goals and objectives of successful procurement planning. More importantly, academics have not produced either normative or descriptive theory that has utility for procurement practitioners. The section closes with an exploration of the implications that the strategic-based approach to procurement planning holds for the development of public sector procurement research. In addition, the foundation for the strategic procurement planning model discussed throughout this book is provided.

Planning in the Public Sector

*A*ll managers, and the organizations where they work, must plan. Planning fulfills several essential functions within an organization (Porter, 1996). First, plans help identify and define the functions and direction in which the organization is heading, assuming that the organization knows where it wants to go. Second, good plans establish decision criteria that service delivery managers can use to guide their decision process, specifically how resources are to be allocated within their units. Third, a well-structured plan provides impetus for performance monitoring and program evaluation. Basically, effective evaluation is not possible without comparison to some predefined benchmark, even if the benchmark is limited to some general notion that benefits should, at a minimum, equal costs. Some plans may even include projected measures of plan performance as well as establish standards to identify failure and judge success. Fourth, the quality and quantity of information that is gathered is limited in the planning process to those things that warrant review. Fifth, effective planning can minimize costs by anticipating workload fluctuations to assign resources more efficiently.

Despite the potential benefits associated with planning, the consensus is that public organizations do little formal planning (Bryson, 1995; Koteen, 1989). A distinction needs to be made between formal and informal planning. Some organizations, and the individuals who are charged with general stewardship, may decide unilaterally where the organization should go and how organizational resources should be used to get there. Under these conditions, very little needs to be formally documented. Undocumented conversations among managers may result in plans, which, again, exist only in individual managers' heads or in the form of scribbled notes. No method for consensus building or stakeholder involvement takes place under informal planning.

Formal planning, on the other hand, is a much more deliberate process for identifying opportunities and threats in the environment and analyzing the organization's particular strengths and weaknesses (Cohen & Eimicke, 1998; Frederickson, 1980). Formal planning is a continuous process which identifies where the organization as a whole, or parts of it, should be going, how it will get there, and, once there, how to evaluate success. At one level a plan may simply describe the activities and tasks that must be carried out within a specific time frame in order to meet specific operational targets. At a much higher level, the plan may seek to define the mission, vision, goals, and objectives, establish performance standards, develop strategies and policies which will enable the organization to adapt, and shape its environment over a period of years. In either case, if events turn out to be different from those that were anticipated, plans will need to be changed.

Strategies, which emanate from formal plans, facilitate organizational learning and adaptation. At some juncture in the past there would have been a statement (typically in the strategic plan or the budget document), which matched these events closely. In reality, stated plans and actual events are unlikely to match exactly—witness September 11, 2001. In addition to strategies which have emerged and have been introduced, there are likely to be expectations and planned possible strategies which have not proved to be viable. However, broad directions can be established and planned and then detailed strategies allowed to emerge as part of an ongoing experiential learning within the organization. Effectively, planning provides an opportunity to integrate a loosely coupled operating system in a systematic manner to ensure that resource allocation decisions are based, in part, on attainment of organizational goals and objectives (Porter, 1996).

Types of Plans

*P*lans may be classified by a host of means. Ranging from strategic plans (organizational plans) to tactical plans (strategies to accomplish strategic goals and objectives). They may be looked at as operational plans, contingency plans, or simply plans. In general, plans may be classified as either standing plans or single-use plans. Both types are used to pursue organizational goals and objectives but in very different ways. Standing plans are used to guide actions that occur over a period of time. There are three principal types of standing plans: policies, procedures, and rules and regulations. Policies are plans that provide general guidance to action. Policies vary from organization to organization, both in scope of subjects covered by policies and how the issues relating to the subject will be treated. Procedures are plans that describe the exact series of actions to be taken in a given situation. Rules and regulations are plans that describe exactly how one particular situation is to be handled (Higgins, 1991).

Single-use plans are plans that are used once and then discarded. In some cases, it may take many years to finish using such plans. In other situations, this plan may be useful for only one day. There are three types of single-use plans: strategies, intermediate plans, and operational or operating plans. The types of planning vary in complexity and cover all levels of management within the organization (Higgins, 1991). Examples of single-use plans include: developing a computerized procurement system, developing an out-sourcing program, developing a material requirements planning (MRP) system with a gradual phase-out of warehouse operations, and developing public works plans to upgrade the organization's infrastructure. Although implementation of the plan may take several years to complete, the plan is still considered to be a single-use plan. When the project is finished, the plan is no longer necessary.

Standing strategic plans are major plans, which commit extensive resources to proposed activities to achieve an organization's major goals and objectives. Strategic planning is complex, more uncertain, and is usually addressed to the entire organization. These plans are concerned with obtaining or leveraging organizational resources to produce meaningful results. Objectives are passed on to middle and lower management who concern themselves to a greater degree with intermediate and operational planning that is intended to implement the strategic plan (Higgins, 1991).

Intermediate plans are plans to help translate strategy into operations. These plans normally commit far fewer organizational resources than do strategies. Operating plans are plans that deal with day-to-day actions, typically for one year or less. Operational plans commit fewer resources than strategies or intermediate plans. Intermediate and operational plans usually cover shorter time spans than strategic planning and are simpler and more certain (Higgins, 1991).

Strategic Planning[1]

*T*his section attempts to synthesize the literature on strategic planning, drawing general conclusions relevant to public sector applications. Attention will be paid to the relationship between procurement planning and strategic planning and the processes that are associated with developing and implementing strategic planning. First, according to Porter (1997), "Strategy is about setting yourself apart from the competition" (p. 17). In this case, "yourself" refers to private sector firms attempting to increase market share. However, in the public sector it is not about market share but, more appropriately, about establishing a plan that voices concerns/needs from the jurisdiction's internal and external environments. Strategic planning is typically depicted as an extremely formal, lengthy, elaborate, and expensive

[1]The authors would like to thank Mr. Tansu Demir for his assistance in researching the information provided in this section. In addition, Mr. Demir provided much of the language used herein.

process, which is only conducted to appease the various stakeholders in the organization. In many cases, these overtly formal and burdensome approaches to strategic planning are inadequate and inflexible to address the dynamic planning needs of today's rapidly changing environment (Slywotzky *et al.* 1999). Further, Hahn and Powers (1999) show that there is no relationship between the level of sophistication involved in the strategic planning process (either through advanced process designs or the utilization of advanced planning techniques) and the impact that strategic planning has on organizational effectiveness and performance.

In contrast to the highly structured strategic planning process, Mintzberg (1993) is quick to suggest that there are other successful approaches to formulating and implementing strategic plans. Mintzberg establishes a planning continuum, where the visionary approach involves one key individual who acts as the catalyst for the organization at the other end of the continuum. Mintzberg suggests a learning approach, which is characterized by continuous cross-organizational cross-functional teamwork. These two alternative approaches reflect the previously identified entrepreneurial approach compared to the synergetic approach proffered in this text. For a number of practitioners and researchers, a planning approach that originates with highly detailed plans and moves progressively to larger concepts is not practical—a bottom-up approach (Russell, 1999). Instead, Russell contends that certain leaders (visionary planners) start with the big picture view (an organizational paradigm) and then move progressively into the details—top-down approach. Regardless of the processes adopted to develop the strategic plan, organizational uniqueness must be considered as a primary determinant. Indeed, Shrader, Taylor, and Dalton (1984) suggest that strategic planning is basically a complex interwoven activity that involves multiple key players across various organizational dimensions. The successful development of the plan requires the identification of an organization's strengths, weaknesses, opportunities, and threats.

A detailed examination of the literature identifying strengths and weakness of each strategic planning approach in the public sector is beyond the intentions of this section. The next chapter will provide a much richer and fully articulated process model for consideration by procurement professionals. However, a brief overview of a conceptual framework common in most strategic planning processes is merited at this juncture (see Figure 1).

According to Fidellow and Hogan (1998), the first action necessary for proper strategic planning is to analyze the organization's mission and/or vision. If these statements currently exist, they should serve as a foundation or focal point of all subsequent planning activities. On the other hand, if a mission or vision

Figure 1 - *Strategic planning framework.*

statement is not currently in place, the articulation of such a statement or statements should precede any further strategic planning processes.

In the public sector, analyzing an existing mission statement or creating a mission statement should serve to focus attention on the overall goals and objectives of the organization. One venue that can be examined, and should be examined, in the development of the mission statement is the enabling legislation that created the organization or agency in the first place. A critical question that must be addressed in the early stages of strategic planning is whether or not the mission statement and vision correctly identify what the government desires to emulate in actual practice and to determine if the goals and aspirations of the organization are in unison with the enabling legislation. If the answer to this question is "no," those charged with articulating the statement should adjust the statement to more accurately align the wants and needs of the government or adjust the processes and practices of existing structures to better align the mission statement with what is occurring in practice. Further, governments should examine and critique their mission and vision statements within the context of their external environments to determine if the statements need to reflect changing preferences.

If a gap were to exist between the mission statement and vision statement and the current and anticipated environmental conditions, consideration should be given to adjusting both to properly reflect current conditions and anticipate change. Producing a mission statement can also serve as a motivating factor to potentially locate various perceptions about the true aspirations of the organization. It can also help identify discrepancies between the organization's current functions and processes and the mission statement. An essential element to effective planning is to evaluate the internal and external environments of the organization (Fidellow & Hogan, 1998). Perhaps the best, and most familiar, way to accomplish this is to assess the organization's strengths, weaknesses, opportunities, and threats (SWOT). The SWOT analysis should be conducted early in the process (Cohen & Eimicke, 1998; Schneider & De Meyer, 1991). SWOT analysis has been offered as an effective means to accomplish what Christensen (1997) refers to as mapping and identifying the driving forces organizations must consider in articulating their missions and visions. Once these forces have been identified, Christensen suggests that individual strategies (manifest in the plan itself) can be isolated that can address these driving forces. Yet, individual strategies must be developed within the identified priorities and current organizational resources. The fulfillment of this process must be headed by time lines to identify key benchmarks and isolate responsibility centers (Fidellow & Hogan, 1998).

From a procurement perspective, the importance of incorporating cross-functional teams/tasks into the overall strategic planning process has been contended by a number of researchers. Basically, research has emphasized the added value of allowing key personnel within the organization to participate in the strategic planning process. By including key stakeholders, the strategic planning process should benefit from the additional knowledge and expertise possessed by these individuals within the organization (Hamel, 1996; Russell, 1999). One potential benefit of involving staff is that some of them may act like champions or advocates for the strategies developed. This, in turn, can potentially reduce the traditional bureaucratic obstacles typically associated with trying to motivate personnel to embrace the strategic planning process when they are not actively involved in the development of the plan. The involvement of key personnel within the organization also included middle management and key stakeholders outside the traditional boundaries of the organization. Oswald, Mossholder, and Harris (1994) found, for example, a positive correlation between the managers' perception of actively participating in the strategic planning process and their associated psychological attachment to the organization. But, in many cases, the involvement of staff or key personnel is seldom sought (Hamel, 1996), and the lack of staff involvement results in poorly defined and implemented strategic plans.

The critical nature of staff involvement, according to Hamel (1996), transcends the organization itself. Hamel further suggests that organizations which are operating in multiple and, in some cases, conflicting environments, need to consider input from all stakeholders, not just those that are external to the organization.

The benefits of staff involvement in this process have been suggested to include improved job satisfaction (Daniels & Bailey, 1999) and lower anxiety about job security (Stimpert & Duhaime, 1997). Ultimately, however, the involvement of internal and external stakeholders does not relinquish senior management of their need to participate. What this implies is that the role of key players in the strategic planning process must assume a more consolatory role in the planning process rather than an autocratic, top-down roll of the past.

Researchers have contended for quite some time now that leadership within the organization must play a central role in aggregating internal and external information that can impact the organization and how this information is to be assimilated into the overall strategic planning process (Cohen & Eimicke, 1998). The idea that staff should be involved in the strategic planning process is particularly relevant in government. By involving staff, the government could receive additional and more accurate information related to the external environment, such as the status of local economic conditions, community concerns, politically sensitive issues, and customer needs and wants. Staff involvement can also enhance service delivery by establishing communication links between diverse members of the service delivery area. Staff members could also provide practical advice regarding the potential strengths or weaknesses associated with certain strategic planning alternatives.

Ultimately, the success of the strategic planning process is manifested in the critical nature of the implementation stage. Remember, any great strategy (or for that matter, any poorly conceived strategy), if not implemented properly, is destined to fail and cause an inordinate amount of angst. Not only is the articulation of the strategic plan important, but the actions that the plan elicits from those charged with carrying out the plan become just as critical. In fact, Mintzberg (1993) strongly suggests that focusing most of the attention on the strategic plan and the planning process itself oftentimes results in poorly implemented strategic plans. Consequently, all good strategic plans are designed with specific attention to individual strategies and associated time lines for implementation to ensure that the plan does not collect dust on someone's bookshelf.

To briefly summarize the literature on strategic planning—and, as anyone knows, this is a rather expansive literature base—the following steps provide a conceptual model that can be used in strategic planning for a government, regardless of size (see Figure 2). Each of the state activities is part and parcel to the overall success of the planning effort. Often, an organization may attempt to bypass a particular activity, but this may lead to plan failure. The process is most effective when it is followed by the entire organization, not just units.

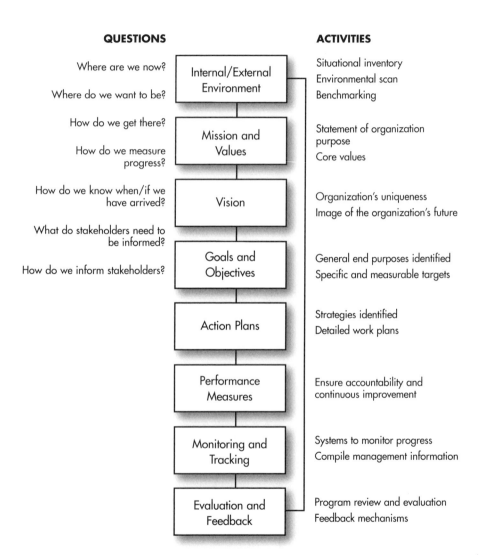

Figure 2 - *Elements of strategic planning: Goals, objectives and performance measures.*

The Role of Procurement in Strategic Planning

*I*n order to understand procurement's role in the overall strategic planning process, the different structural/functional relationships procurement can manifest within organizations need to be examined. Traditionally, public organizations have been considered hierarchal, where functional authority and accountability are products of the division of labor. Structural roles are that of service, staff, or line function. A service role is one in which a designated unit relieves the rest of an organization from performing a function that is common to all units within the organization. In the past, public procurement has been regarded primarily as a service function catering to the individual needs of service delivery managers. In this capacity, the procurement department focuses on:

- providing a cohesive organized operation which delivers adequate and timely material support to service delivery managers;

- furnishing material and service support in a tactful and courteous manner;

- receiving advice from competent personnel in all departments;

- maintaining good relationships with all personnel in all departments;

- making efforts to ensure that the using departments are informed of each other's needs, problems, and benefits contributed by purchasing to the jurisdiction; and

- keeping in mind that the purchasing department is continuing to maintain its service function.

In addition to the service function, procurement plays a staff function. A staff function is typically one that provides information to affected groups within the organization—both strategic and tactical. Recent trends in both the private and public sectors have encouraged the procurement department to take on expanded staff functions as well as continuing its service role. In fulfilling the staff function, procurement is responsible for advising management and user agencies on such matters as:

- general market conditions;

- new products and services which may be used to the organization's advantage or disadvantage;

- changes, trends, and availability of specific products and services commonly used by the organization;

- opportunities for establishing and improving relationships with product suppliers, service providers, and professional consultants; and
- new policies, regulations, or any legislation necessary to facilitate the procurement function.

A line function is one in which the department has clearly defined operational responsibilities and authority where it contributes to the organization's bottom line. In the case of government, the bottom line is represented by service to the taxpayer. For service level functions, like procurement, the line authority emanates primarily within the function, having no direct authority over other functions. Other line agencies, like public safety and recreation, report directly to a chief administrative officer and have clearly identified channels of communication and responsibility.

Purchasing...should have clearly defined responsibilities

Another way to look at the role of procurement in determining the best way to allocate organizational resources is to isolate where procurement reports within the hierarchy of organizational power. Reporting is an indication of the status of a department and is a clear key to procurement's influence within the organization. The higher in the organizational hierarchy purchasing reports, the more authority and responsibility it will carry. Purchasing needs the functional authorities and should have clearly defined responsibilities in such areas as:

- strategic planning;
- budget preparation;
- specifications and requisition development;
- purchasing and source selection;
- receiving goods, inspection, and quality control; and
- stores control and distribution.

Only recently has procurement's role in the organization's planning process been recognized (Boyd, 1994). Management has realized that effective procurement can impact a jurisdiction's ability to deliver the needed services to demanding taxpayers. In proactive procurement, professionals plan for and initiate action. In reactive purchasing, practitioners merely respond to the demands placed upon them. The following factors influence whether procurement plays a proactive or reactive role in the planning process:

- the degree of sophistication in the jurisdictional planning process;
- how dependent the jurisdiction is on procured goods and services;
- how the procurement function is viewed by top management;
- the state of evolutionary development of the procurement function within the jurisdiction; and
- the ability of the procurement professional to shift from a tactical to a strategic role in the resource allocation process.

Any one of these factors can significantly impact the contributions procurement makes to the planning process.

In addition to the structural roles that procurement can assume, McCue and Pitzer (2000) note that procurement serves three essential purposes: *control, management,* and *planning.* To a large extent, the potential impact that procurement will have on the resource allocation process will depend on which, if any, of these purposes are stressed within an organization. For example, when organizations focus on control, procurement's main thrust is to ensure that resources are allocated consistent with established policy (normally manifest in the budget document) and that no resources are used for fraudulent purposes (normally determined during an audit). Historically, control within the procurement process has been maintained by a hierarchal system that emphasizes accountability, constraining individual behavior, and locating authority in the hands of those charged with the responsibility of conducting a particular procurement activity.

If, as reform efforts suggest (Gore, 1993), the control system is decentralized, fixing accountability and maintaining control of purchasing processes may be compromised, if service and sub-service delivery managers are responsible for maintaining and choosing the goods and services that are to be consumed, when they are to be consumed, and by whom they are going to be consumed. In order for control to be developed, service delivery managers must posses the requisite skills and knowledge to execute public policy. When control (concentration of power through "red tape") is decentralized to service delivery managers so that they can be more responsive and adaptive to their environments, it is presumed that those invested in the control: are to act in the best interest of the government; are sufficiently knowledgeable about the particulars associated with specific regulations; and that the system can provide the support to perform procurement functions within established purchasing policies and procedures. In contrast, a central procurement authority attempts to facilitate service delivery managers' potential needs within a system that values control and compliance with law and policy.

Procurement also exercises a control function through strict adherence to legal, professional, and administrative requirements that define the purchasing process. Service managers often view this control function as a constraint on the purchasing agency's service support responsibilities (McCue & Pitzer, 2000). Although purchasing agencies support service agencies, service managers exercise no authority over the purchasing agency. Otherwise its control function could be compromised (Gianakis & McCue, 2000).

Procurement also performs a management support function as well as a control function. Procurement provides support to service delivery agencies by providing them with the goods and services they require to pursue their missions. In this capacity, procurement attempts to minimize costs by aggregating requests to take advantage of volume prices, develop knowledge of markets, shop for lowest prices, maintain adequate inventories, and build expertise. Procurement can provide managers with various alternatives to their current vendors, project changes in the market for specific goods and services, help managers reduce costs, and provide decision makers with alternative decision criteria (McCue & Pitzer, 2000).

Procurement planning in the public sector includes both strategic and tactical components. Strategic-level planning is long-range planning and is typically performed annually, when organizations need to expand their capacities to address growing community concerns. Tactical-level planning involves supply planning, which primarily includes the optimization of the flow of goods and services through an organization. Decisions at this level include which services must be produced and in what quantity, who is to produce them (make or buy decisions), what supply sources are available or need to be developed to facilitate anticipated needs, and scheduling of activities.

From the long-range perspective, the scope of the strategic procurement planning process is extremely broad and comprehensive, touching on all aspects of organizational support and taking place in three distinct zones. The *agency zone* is where service delivery manager requirements for the provision of goods or services originate and where funding allocations for those requirements are managed. In large agencies, this zone may include personnel who hold inventory; initiate call-ups or orders directly to suppliers using pre-arranged mechanisms, such as blanket purchase orders or standing offers; or send requisitions to the purchasing agency for review and approval. The *supplier zone* is where the producer (the provider of required goods and services) resides. There is a continuing interaction with the supplier that extends far beyond the simple satisfaction of a requirement. Such interaction may come directly from the end-user in the case of scheduling issues or shipment inquiries; it may come from purchasing staff in the transmission of initial orders, amendment of orders and delivery expedition, and payment. Of course, within the *management zone* itself, procurement interacts not only with clients and suppliers but also with other purchasing people in the organization to ensure service support, as well as staffing, budgeting, and managerial decision making.

The Public Sector Procurement Cycle

A starting point for the delineation of the strategic procurement model in government, specifically for state and local governments, is identified in the foundation text, *Public Procurement Management* (2000), produced by the National Institute of Governmental Purchasing (NIGP). This book establishes the knowledge framework driving the procurement profession, as well as provides the conceptual boundaries necessary for certification requirements at both the buyers (Certified Professional Public Buyer) and officers levels (Certified Public Purchasing Officer). Figure 3 provides the basis of the process identified by NIGP (1998, p. 8). As Figure 3 shows, the purchasing cycle consists of three phases. Phase 1 is the creation of the purchasing plan and the associated scheduling necessary to accomplish specific tasks. Within this phase, budgeting, needs assessment, specifications identification, and project management are conducted by staff within their respective agencies. Purchasing facilitates the planning and scheduling requirements by assisting in identifying market segmentation and related product information, advising end-users of the legal and policy environment of purchasing, and building good will. We assume good will is exhibited between the purchasing agency and the various service delivery organizations within the jurisdiction. Otherwise, procurement's control function may be questioned.

The second phase of the purchasing cycle is supplier selection. According to NIGP, the purchasing agency is responsible for all of the activities identified in this phase. This does not preclude the utilization of various arrangements to select a supplier, but the ultimate responsibility of the selection process rests with purchasing. Activities associated with supplier selections include: determining the purchasing method (bids, proposals, etc.), preparing the solicitation document, receiving bids/proposals, tabulating and evaluating bids/proposals, and preparing the contract.

Contract administration is the final phase of the purchasing process. This phase consists of the receipt and disposal (in those instances where disposal is a viable option) and contract payment, where the responsibility of contract payment is in the finance/treasury department.

	Activity	Who is responsible?	Who assists?
Planning/ Scheduling	Budgeting	End User	Finance, Purchasing
	Identify need	End User	
	Determine specifications	End User	Purchasing Supplier Community
	Advise on market conditions	Purchasing	
	Recommend substitute products	Purchasing	
	Recommend new products/services	Purchasing	
	Build goodwill	Purchasing	
	Advise on policy/ regulation/legislation	Purchasing	
	Initiate requisition	End User	Purchasing
	Project Management	End User	Purchasing
Select Supplier	Check excess stock	Purchasing	
	Determine method of purchase	Purchasing	
	Prepare solicitation/ sourcing	Purchasing	
	Receive bids/proposals	Purchasing	
	Tabulate bids	Purchasing	
	Evaluate proposals	Purchasing	End User
	Prepare contract	Purchasing	End User
Administer Contract	Receipt	End User	Purchasing
	Payment	Finance	
	Amend contract	Purchasing	
	Disposal	Purchasing	End User

Figure 3 - *NIGP's purchasing cycle.*

CIPS Purchasing & Supply Management (P&SM) Model

This illustrates the generic P&SM processes and how they contribute to any organisation

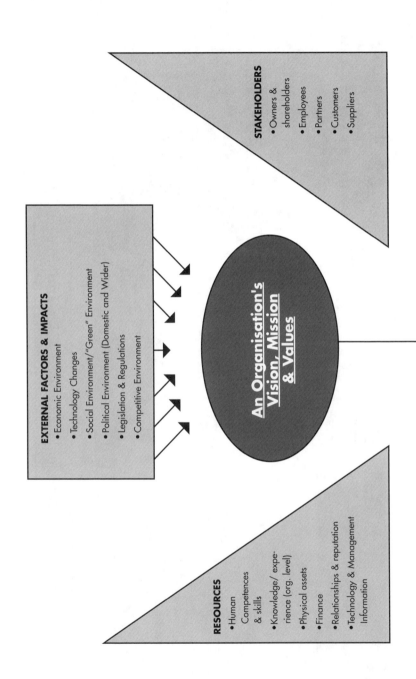

EXTERNAL FACTORS & IMPACTS
- Economic Environment
- Technology Changes
- Social Environment/"Green" Environment
- Political Environment (Domestic and Wider)
- Legislation & Regulations
- Competitive Environment

An Organisation's Vision, Mission & Values

STAKEHOLDERS
- Owners & shareholders
- Employees
- Partners
- Customers
- Suppliers

RESOURCES
- Human Competences & skills
- Knowledge/experience (org. level)
- Physical assets
- Finance
- Relationships & reputation
- Technology & Management Information

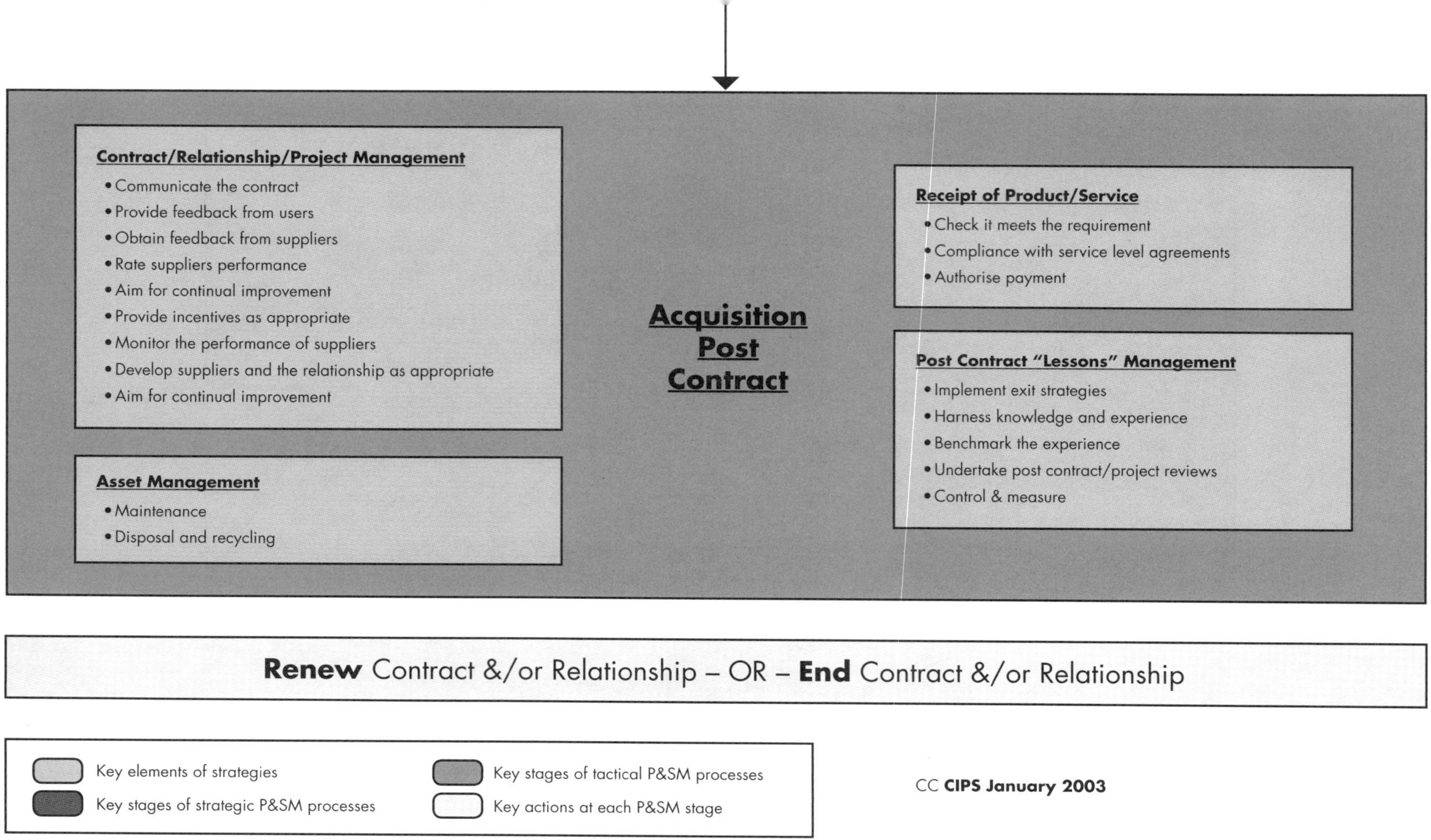

Contract/Relationship/Project Management

• Communicate the contract
• Provide feedback from users
• Obtain feedback from suppliers
• Rate suppliers performance
• Aim for continual improvement
• Provide incentives as appropriate
• Monitor the performance of suppliers
• Develop suppliers and the relationship as appropriate
• Aim for continual improvement

Asset Management

• Maintenance
• Disposal and recycling

**Acquisition
Post
Contract**

Receipt of Product/Service

• Check it meets the requirement
• Compliance with service level agreements
• Authorise payment

Post Contract "Lessons" Management

• Implement exit strategies
• Harness knowledge and experience
• Benchmark the experience
• Undertake post contract/project reviews
• Control & measure

Renew Contract &/or Relationship – OR – **End** Contract &/or Relationship

CC **CIPS January 2003**

Key elements of strategies

Key stages of strategic P&SM processes

Key stages of tactical P&SM processes

Key actions at each P&SM stage

Figure 4 - *CIPS Purchasing and supply management (P&SM) Model*

Recently, the Chartered Institute of Purchasing and Supply (CIPS) developed their own model of the procurement cycle. Its model specifically mentions planning as a component of the purchasing cycle (CIPS, 2002). Although one can contend that CIPS provides a robust depiction of the procurement cycle, there are a number of limitations that must be discussed regarding the nature and placement of the planning process. As Figure 4 suggests, CIPS posits that procurement planning takes place long after the mission, vision, goals, and objectives of the organization have been identified. Once again, if this is the case, then purchasing simply becomes a reactive service agency that attempts to add value to the allocation of organizational resources, once a determination has been made elsewhere. There is validity in this contention, just as there is validity in NIGP's historical perception of the public sector purchasing cycle. As evidenced by this text, NIGP recognizes that procurement planning takes place concurrently, while strategy, goals, and objectives are identified.

Thai (2001) provides an overview of the various purchasing process models that have been offered in the past. In addition, he proposes his own systems view of procurement. As Figure 5 indicates, Thai captures the integrative nature of the process, highlighting the relationship between procurement and its environments. Further, the continuous nature of the systems approach he adopted suggests that procurement is neither static nor closed; but, like the historical perspectives of NIGP and CIPS, there is no mention of the potential impact of planning and procurement's potential role in the planning process. He simply states the need for procurement planning. In all cases, each model failed to suggest the critical nature of systems integration and did not suggest that procurement should be at the strategic planning table. This is why the various sub-systems within the organization fail to meet organizational goals and objectives. When integration of the various planning levels becomes mani-fest, then, and only then, procurement can become a functional contributor to the effective and efficient allocation of organizational resources.

The procurement process models highlighted above provide realistic views of procurement's role/involvement in organizational decision making. This does not suggest that the purchasing frameworks identified either formerly by NIGP, currently by CIPS, or Thai's conceptual model is poorly conceived or lacks merit; rather, it suggests that the procurement cycle offered herein expands upon those models and provides a more robust and integrated strategic approach to public sector procurement, reminiscent of the value-chain man-agement model utilized in the private sector. In many situations, "value chain" and "supply chain" are used interchangeably, but there is a difference between the two concepts worth noting. According to Lamming (1993), supply chain management primarily focuses on all activities which make the manufacturing process operate efficiently. Value-chain management, on the other hand, focuses on each step of the process, ranging from the acquisition of raw materials all the way to the satisfaction of customers. The objective of value-chain management is to effectively deliver value to end-users at the least possible total cost. As identified herein, and within these conceptual frameworks discussed, supply-chain management must be a sub-set of value-chain management.

Just as the supply-chain is a sub-set of the value-chain process, the value-chain is a sub-set of the strategic procurement planning process. Procurement planning, in turn, is a sub-set of the strategic planning process of the organization, which is the essence of the organizational resource allocation process. Specifically, strategic procurement looks at the entire value-adding process in the context of facilitating the attainment of organizational mission, goals, and objectives. Just optimizing each individual step in the value-chain may not be the entire answer in the public sector. Public sector procurement has a number of unique dimensions competing for public resources. In public sector value-chain management, if you choose a less expensive bid package by negotiating

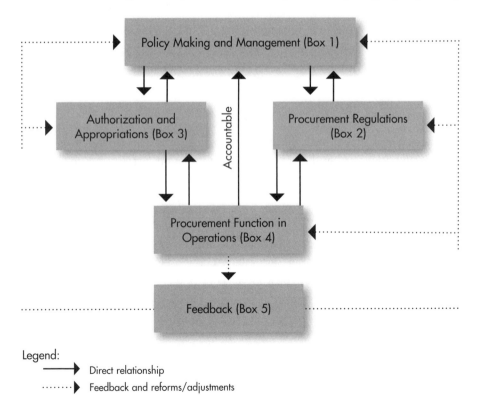

Figure 5 - *Public procurement system.*

with a supplier, you may be detracting from the total value of the product; that is, if value is placed on competition and access over costs. Negotiating with suppliers may reduce final costs and increase value to the end-user; but, if the negotiations also inhibit or reduce other supplier access—a presumed goal of public sector procurement—the value to the organization may simply be reduced costs rather that increased access and minority participation. In the private sector, this value may be manifest in reduced costs; but, in the public sector, reduced costs are not the only determinant in making such resource allocation decisions.

The strategic procurement approach takes the value-chain approach to a different level. Instead of limiting procurement to the satisfaction of a requirement identified elsewhere or to implement optimization decisions made at the sub-system level, where conflict may arise in meeting organizational goals, strategic procurement places procurement at the forefront of the organizational resource allocation process. Not only should procurement be concerned with the impact of the value-chain on the management of resources within the organization, but procurement must, in the first place, be concerned with the legitimacy of the value-chain in the strategic position of the organization. Questions to be asked include:

- What is the right good or service?
- Do we need the items in the first place?
- What vendors should be contacted and why?
- What strategic advantage does this procurement have relative to the attainment of a specific organizational goal or objective?

These and other such questions are critical dimensions of relating the value-chain to the strategic position of the organization in the public sector and, ultimately to the effective and efficient delivery of public services.

Frequently, value-chain management is conducted in a vacuum. A number of optimizing efforts fail in the near – or – long-term, because they are not linked to either the organization's strategic plans or agency/department functional plans; and these, in turn, are not linked to the procurement plan, which, in turn, is not linked to the allocation process (strategic position) of the organization. A public organization may have the best intentions to use value-chain management to increase the effectiveness and efficiency by which goods and services are delivered to the citizens. Unfortunately, the sub-systems that make up the system are often neglected in value-chain management. Say, for example, a government spends the next two years conducting a strategic planning effort. During this time, elected officials and key individuals/stakeholders are contacted, and various planning documents are produced articulating the mission, vision, and goals and objectives for the organization. In some cases, particularly at the federal level, a typical response by departments is to facilitate the strategic planning effort by identifying goals and objectives within their programmatic areas, with no firm intention or dedication to the achievement of these goals and objectives. In some cases, these are simply given "lip-service." In other cases, agencies may earnestly attempt to facilitate the attainment of specific goals and objectives, but there has been no agency planning effort to support the overall strategic effort.

Even in situations where the agency may attempt to facilitate the attainment of organizational goals and objectives, the organizational support systems may fail to integrate their planning efforts into that of the agency's and the overall organizational planning. The planning effort begins to resemble a loosely-coupled system manifest at the federal level (Gianakis & McCue, 2000; Thai, 2001). Service activities, like finance, human resource management, asset management, and procurement, must all be on the same planning page for the process to work effectively in the public sector. When variances occur, there must be methods to remedy the variance and strategic management efforts to correct the actions. If they are allowed to continue, the strategic position of the organization will be challenged.

An Integrated Procurement Planning Model

*T*he model proposed herein (Figure 6) is based on the assumption that procurement is a continuous—although in some cases, disjointed—process for allocating organizational resources. Not to minimize the role of finance or budgeting, human resource management, or other support systems in decisions affecting the allocation process—as we know, these areas have received far more attention in the literature than procurement—ultimately, these functions are the support systems for managing and controlling the acquisition and production of goods and services (even human capital) that are consumed in the development and delivery of products and services to the public. The process of assigning organizational resources (i.e., procuring goods and services) to various organizational decisions are procurement decisions—not finance, not budgeting (although

Public sector procurement can no longer afford to remain in the resource allocation "closet".

budgeting is considered the main process for allocating organizational resources), or human resource management.

Public sector procurement can no longer afford to remain in the resource allocation "closet." Procurement professionals must become intimately involved in allocation decisions but not after decisions have been made, as suggested by NIGP and CIPS, but they must become important players at the strategy table. Take, for instance, a situation where a government is deciding to either build a new school or expand an existing school. The first question one must ask is: Why is this question being considered in the first place? For the sake of this example, lets assume that demographic trends collected by the local school board indicated that overcrowding at the local school will reach a critical point within the next five years. In order to rationalize the decision sequence for determining which option to choose, the costs of each alternative must be estimated. What typically happens is that the individuals involved in the decision-making sequence ask for cost figures to be computed for each alternative. At this point, the purchasing department may or may not become involved in the planning process. Most typically, it is not.

What the conceptual model offered in this book demands is that procurement should have been at the decision-making table in the first place. A central component of in the private sector is market segmentation to advance a firm's

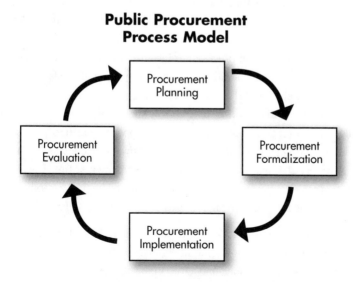

Public Procurement Process Model

Figure 6 - *Public procurement process model.*

competitive advantage. If procurement were to consider market segments, e.g., clients in the private sector, there would have been ample indication that the demographic composition of the community was changing. Knowing the potential impact that these demographic changes would have on the products and services of the government, it would have been malfeasance of the procurement professional to not anticipate the potential ramifications of these "segmental" shifts. If a private sector organization did not capture these changes, they would lose the competitive advantage. If the demographic shifts were sufficiently large, it could ultimately result in organizational closure.

The next step in the planning process is to determine what materials and services are to be purchased. Responsibility for this determination varies with the requirement, as will be discussed in Chapter 5. In many cases, the using department is responsible. For example, Plant Engineering is responsible for developing equipment requirements. Plant Operations develops requirements for operating supplies, such as drill bits, lubricating oils, and related items. Administrative Services initiates requirements for office supplies, equipment, and services. The responsibility for determining which component materials to specify for newly designed services is a complex issue, complicated by the frequently conflicting interests, orientations, and biases of the many departments that have an interest in the end item or service. In this case, procurement can be an objective abettor in requirement determination.

Historically, procurement's contribution to the organization's success has been viewed primarily as ensuring the timely availability of required supplies and services, obtaining them at economical prices and at the right time. However, these contributions are greatly expanded, when procurement is included at the beginning of the design process. For instance, as material requirements are developed, procurement should ensure that only essential needs are incorporated in the requirement. The description of the requirement, usually a specification (as will be discussed in Chapter 6), should not contain features that unduly limit competition among qualified suppliers. Further, procurement can help the designer to be sensitive to the relative availability and cost of the alternative materials that may satisfy product requirements. Timely availability of required materials and services usually is enhanced by the availability of two or more qualified vendors or carefully structured strategic alliances.

Before we touch upon the phases of the procurement cycle identified in Figure 6, it is imperative that we note the integrative nature of the cycle. Planning, formalization, administration, and evaluation are not stand-alone activities. During the origination of the cycle, planning consists of identifying or modifying procurement goals and objectives. This stems from changes in demand, the market, laws, and policies. Once a plan is established, the next stage begins the formalization of the plan, either through statutory or institutional policies and processes. At this juncture, some of the goals and objectives identified in the plan may be altered as a result of shifting political sentiment, resource constraints, or other environmental reasons. Also, this stage helps identify strategies that are to be used to achieve the goals and objectives, as well as the resources that are to be consumed in the achievement of the objectives. The administration phase ensures that the plan is carried out consistent with the strategies identified in the formalization process. Variances from the original plan must be identified and evaluated to document changes and to identify potential bottlenecks in the process. Finally, the overall plan must be evaluated in some objective manner. The product of the cycle acts as input to the next round of procurement planning, setting the table, if you will, for the planning process anew.

The first phase of the procurement cycle is the planning phase. The planning and analysis phase takes place at the beginning of the cycle, but analysis does occur at other periods in the cycle. The phase consists of documenting and analyzing the environment of the procurement function: evaluating the strengths, weaknesses, opportunities, and threats to the procurement process, and identifying key stakeholders of the procurement process. Once these factors are examined, the planning stage articulates a set of goals and objectives to be accomplished in the time identified.

Procurement formalization emerges from the synthesis of organizational and purchasing goals with the various environmental constraints that impinge on the total planning system. In short, procurement strategy formulation serves to structure the various problems confronting the procurement decision process. Given that there are limited resources which can be brought to bear on particular purchasing-related problems, the process of strategy formulation forces the procurement professional to select from among a number of options and focus on a more manageable array of alternative courses of action. Unfortunately, with the exception of life-cycle analysis, there are few analytical tools which purchasing managers can utilize to help frame their strategic options; hence, the need for theory development.

Despite this difficulty, one can envision hierarchies of strategies that will help procurement professionals structure the procurement planning process more effectively. Each set of strategies, at different levels within the hierarchy, would have a particular management focus requiring different types of environmental information, and each would have a unique set of performance criteria. Operationally, strategic development would proceed in a progressive, step-like fashion. That is, successful attainment of lower level strategies would be necessary before higher-level strategies could be enacted.

From the identification of goals and objectives, the lowest level of the procurement planning and formalization process would be comprised of performance-related strategies. These strategies focus primarily on managing purchasing resources, controlling expenses, and serving users' needs within the organization. Mid levels in the hierarchy would contain systems-related strategies. These strategies encompass issues relevant to vendor analysis, inventory management, value analysis, and other strategies that serve to coordinate various organizational sub-systems. Client/customer-related strategies would be found at the highest level. These strategies focus on the buyer's intrinsic bargaining power, which generates purchasing leverage and, as a result, enhances the allocative efficiency and effectiveness of the organization. Key issues center on understanding the structure of the supplying market; the impact of multinational sourcing on product costs; the optimal level of vertical integration; and other methods for creating maximum leverage with chosen suppliers.

At its core, procurement administration is an implementation task. Three types of administrative tools can be utilized to implement strategic plans. Broadly classified, they fit in the categories of structure, process, and behavior. Structure entails organizational design issues, which affect coordination, delegation of authority, communications flows, and task responsibility—both within the procurement department and between procurement and other departments. For instance, the execution of competitive procurement strategies can be enhanced by a less bureaucratic, more informal, more adaptable organizational structure. Process refers to such control mechanisms as resource allocation sub-systems, the evaluation system, and the rewards and sanctions system. One would expect, for example, that performance-related strategies would have more tangible, easily measured evaluative criteria than either of the other hierarchical strategies. For instance, the results achieved through a cost reduction program are more immediately discernible than are the benefits produced by nurturing long-term, stable supplier relationships. Finally, behavior focuses on the interpersonal skills and managerial styles employed by procurement professionals to achieve their particular strategic plans.

The process of procurement evaluation brings the planning process full circle and forces managers to confront the appropriateness of potential strategic sourcing alternatives. For the procurement manager, the objective is to understand both the process and the results of strategic procurement planning. Some of the most relevant evaluative questions that should be addressed include:

- Are the procurement strategies mutually achievable?
- Do they address strategic goals and objectives?
- Do they reinforce each other? Is there synergy?
- Do the strategies focus on crucial procurement issues?
- Do the purchasing strategies exploit environmental opportunities?
- Do they deal with external threats?
- Can the strategies be carried out in light of resource constraints?
- Is the timing consistent with the department and/or organization's ability to adapt to the change?
- Are the strategies understood by key implementers?
- Is there organizational commitment? Is there sufficient managerial capability/talent to support effective procurement planning?

In short, the dominant concern throughout the process focuses on the effective allocation of organizational and procurement resources that addresses environmental constraints and opportunities.

Conclusion

*T*he times, as the song says, they are a changing. So, too, are the times changing for public procurement professionals confronting emerging technologies, calls for procurement reform, and various budgetary and institutional constraints on operational resources. It is time for procurement to take the lead in the resource allocation process of governments. This chapter has attempted to identify a conceptual model that places procurement at the forefront of organizational decision making. The model suggests that the allocative efficiency of public organizations will never be efficient or effective without the integration of the various sub-systems that make up the organization. If these loosely coupled systems continue to operate in a vacuum—as functional silos—and if procurement continues to deny its strategic importance, then citizens will continue to receive less than optimal goods and services.

One of the major reasons that public sector procurement has not received the same level of recognition as its private sector counterparts has been, in part, due to the limited perspective the profession has of itself. One of the major weaknesses of the purchasing framework offered by the NIGP, historically speaking, is the belief that purchasing does not get involved in any form of planning. This has limited the strategic position of the planning function and will continue to impact the obtainment of strategic goals and objectives as long as these sub-systems are not integrated into the more strategic position of the organization. According to Figure 2, the planning component of the acquisition process rests purely in the hands of the originating department, finance, and other key decision makers in the organization. The fact that procurement is not present at this critical stage is troublesome. The CIPS model attempts to leverage procurement planning but positions the planning process well after identifying organizational goals and objectives. This, too, is problematic. For the public organization to effectively manage organizational resources, the procurement process must be engaged early in the planning process.

The procurement cycle proposed in this book builds upon the framework identified by the NIGP, the CIPS, and Thai by including a more robust, although conceptually parsimonious, approach to procurement than has been previously posited. The strategic-based approach to procurement includes: planning, formalization, implementation, and evaluation and feedback—similar to the purchasing systems model identified by McCue and Pitzer (2000). When procurement is viewed in light of its control, management, and planning function, and when the procurement system is divided into the supplier, agency, and management dimensions, one can readily see how and why procurement must become an essential partner in the strategic planning process of the organization. What has traditionally limited procurement's assent to organizational resource allocations decisions is that the link between the strategic planning process and the procurement planning process has often been neglected. If the various organizational sub-systems fail to support the system's goals and objectives, as is often the case in government, then a mismatch will occur; resources will be under utilized or incorrectly utilized; and service delivery managers will respond by maintaining and acting as loosely-coupled systems. Only when all sub-systems support the system can the organization fulfill its mission.

In this book, we do not attempt to fully articulate the procurement cycle but, instead, focus on the primary planning and formalization components, which are discussed in the following chapters. Other texts in this series will develop the other substantive areas in more detail. For example, implementation issues will be addressed by the text on contract management, while formalization issues will be discussed in the solicitation text. We will build on Figure 5 in the following chapters by presenting the various components of the cycle relative to planning activities associated with each phase.

References

Boyd, R. (1994). *Purchasing in the year 2000: The next evolution.* Presented at the 79th Annual Purchasing Conference, Tempe, Arizona.

Briggs, S., & Keogh, W. (1999). Integrating human resource strategy and strategic planning to achieve business excellence. *Total Quality Management, 10,* 447-453.

Bryson, J. M. (1995). *Strategic planning for public and nonprofit organizations: A guide strengthening and sustaining organizational achievement.* San Francisco: Jossey-Bass.

Charter Institute of Purchasing and Supplies (2003). *CIPS Purchasing & Supply Management (P&SM Model).* Lincolnshire, UK.

Christensen, C. M. (1997). Making strategy: Learning by doing. *Harvard Business Review, 75,* 141-150.

Cohen, S., & Eimicke, W. (1998). *Tools for innovators: Creative strategies for managing public sector organizations.* San Francisco: Jossey-Bass.

Daniels, K., & Bailey, A. (1999). Strategy development processes and participation in decision making: predictors of role stressors and job satisfaction. *Journal of Applied Management Studies, 8,* 27-42.

Ferguson, W. C., Hartley, M. F., Turner, G. B., & Pierce, E. M. (1996). Purchasing's role in corporate strategic planning. *International Journal of Physical Distribution and Logistics Management, 26* (4) 51-62.

Fidellow, J. A., & Hogan, M. (1998). Strategic planning: Implementing a foundation. *Nursing Management, 29,* 34-36.

Frederickson, G. H. (1980). *New public administration.* Tuscaloosa: The University of Alabama Press.

Gadde, L., & Hakansson, H. (1994). The changing role of purchasing: Reconsidering three strategic issues. *European Journal of Purchasing and Supply Management, 1*(1) 27-35.

Gianakis, G. A., & McCue, C. P. (1999). *Local government budgeting: A managerial perspective.* Westport, CT: Quorum Books (hard-cover), Praeger Publishing (paperback).

Gianakis, G., & Wang, X. (2000). Decentralizing the purchasing function in municipal governments: A national survey. *Journal of Public Budgeting, Accounting and Financial Management, 12*(2) 421-440.

Glueck, W. F., & Jauch, L. R. (1984). *Strategic management and business policy.* New York: McGraw-Hill, Inc.

Gore, A. (1993). *Creating a government that works better and costs less: Report of the National Performance Review.* Washington, DC: U.S. Government Printing Office.

Hahn, W., & Powers, T. (1999). The impact of planning sophistication and implementation on firm performance, *The Journal of Business and Economic Studies, 5,* 19-35.

Haines, S. G. (2000). *The systems thinking approach to strategic planning and management.* Boca Raton, FL: St. Lucie Press.

Hamel, G. (1996). Strategy as revolution. *Harvard Business Review, 74,* 69-80.

Humphreys, P., McIvor, P., & McAleer, E. (1998). The purchasing function as a professional service firm: Implications for training and development. *Journal of European Industrial Training, 22*(1), 3-11.

Kaplan, R. S., & Norton, D. (1992, January-February). The balanced scorecard—Measures that drive performance. *Harvard Business Review,* 71-79.

Koteen, J. (1989). *Strategic management in public and nonprofit organizations: Thinking and acting strategically on public concerns.* New York: Praeger.

Lamming, R. (1993). *Beyond partnership: Strategies for innovation and lean supply.* Hemel, NJ: Prentice-Hall.

Macbeth, D., & Ferguson, N. (1994). *Partnership sourcing: An integrated supply chain approach.* London: Pitman Publishing, Inc.

MacManus, S. (1992). *Doing business with government: Federal, state, local and foreign government purchasing practices for every business and public institution.* New York: Paragon House.

McCue, C. P., & Pitzer, J. T. (2000). Centralized vs. decentralized purchasing: Current trends in governmental procurement practices. *Journal of Public Budgeting, Accounting & Financial Management, 12*(3), 400-420.

McCue, C. P. (2001). Organizing the public purchasing function: A survey of cities and county governments. *Government Finance Review,* 1-5.

McCue, C. P., & Gerasimos A. (2001). Public purchasing: Who's minding the store? *Journal of Public Procurement, 1*(1) 71-96.

Mintzberg, H. (1993). The pitfalls of strategic planning. *California Management Review, 36,* 32-47.

National Institute of Governmental Purchasing (NIGP) (1998). *General public procurement.* Herndon, VA: National Institute of Governmental Purchasing.

National Institute of Governmental Purchasing (NIGP) (2000). *Job analysis.* Herndon, VA: National Institute of Governmental Purchasing.

National Institute of Governmental Purchasing (NIGP) (2000). *Public procurement management.* Herndon, VA: National Institute of Governmental Purchasing.

Osborne, D., & Gaebler, T. (1992). *Reinventing government.* New York: Addison-Wesley.

Osborne, D., & Plastrik, P. (1997). *Banishing bureaucracy: The five strategies for reinventing government.* New York: Addison-Wesley.

Oswald, S. L., Mossholder, K. W., & Harris, S. G. (1994). Vision salience and strategic involvement: Implications for psychological attachment to organization and job. *Strategic Management Journal, 15,* 477-489.

Porter, M. E. (1996). What is strategy? *Harvard Business Review, 74*(4), 61-78.

Porter, M. E. (1997). Creative advantage. *Executive Excellence, 14,* 17-18.

Quayle M., & Quayle, S. (2000). The impact of strategic procurement in the UK further and higher education sectors. *The International Journal of Public Sector Management, 13*(3), 260-284.

Russell, L. (1999). Painting the future picture: Changing and organizing by moving beyond the comfort zone. *Health Forum Journal, 42,* 46-50.

Saunders, M. (1994). *Strategic purchasing and supply chain management.* London: Pitman Publishing, Inc.

Schneider, S. C., & DeMeyer, A. (1991). Interpreting and responding to strategic issues: The impact of national culture. *Strategic Management Journal, 12,* 307-320.

Schreyög G., & Steinmann, H. (1987). Strategic control: A new perspective. *Academy of Management Review, 12*(1), 91-103.

Shrader, C. B., Taylor, L., & Dalton, D. R. (1984). Strategic planning and organizational performance. *Journal of Management, 10,* 149-171.

Slywotzky, A. J., Mundt, K. A., & Quella, J. A. (1999). Pattern thinking. *Management Review, 88,* 32-37.

Spekman, R. E., Kamauff, J. W., & Salmond, D. J. (1994). At last, purchasing is becoming strategic. *Long Range Planning, 27*(2), 76-84.

Stimpert, J. L., & Duhaime, I. M. (1997). Seeing the big picture: The influence of industry, diversification, and business strategy on performance. *Academy of Management Journal, 40,* 560-583.

Taylor, B., & Hussey, D. E. (1982). *The realities of planning.* New York: Pergamon Press.

Thai, K. V. (2001). Public procurement reexamined. *Journal of Public Procurement, 1,* 9-50.

Thompson, M. (1996). Effective purchasing strategy. *Supply Chain Management, 1*(3), 6-8.

Watts, C., Kim, K. Y., & Hahn, C. (1992, Fall). Linking purchasing to corporate competitive strategy. *International Journal of Purchasing and Material Management,* 2-8.

Wheatley, M. (1998, December). Strategic procurement: The route to big savings. *Management Today,* 2-5.

Wildavsky, A. (1984). *The politics of the budgetary process.* Boston: Little, Brown and Company.

CHAPTER 2

Strategic Planning in the Public Sector

O ver the last decades a number of governments have faced various attempts to re-engineer business processes, implement total quality management systems, and adopt other popular transformational initiatives that have not lived up to their original hype (McHugh, 1997). The purpose of a number of these reform efforts was to make government more customer-friendly and customer-focused (Gore, 1993). Along with this new awareness of "customers," government was forced to accomplish these new initiatives more efficiently—with either the same amount of resources or, as is most often the case, with decreased resources. Such an emphasis can obviously be appropriate and effective where the organization is confident that it knows what it is doing is right, for now as well as for the future. As Spekman (1989) states, periodically, there is a need to revisit original aims and objectives of the organization to ensure that it is "doing the right things" as well as "doing them right." Re-enter strategic planning (Demos, Chung, & Beck, 2001).

Strategic planning has been around for centuries, particularly in the form of intelligence gathering for military purposes. In terms of strategic planning for organizations, Ellram and Carr (1994) contend that strategic planning can be traced back to the Harvard Policy Model, which was published in the 1920s by the Harvard Business School. They suggest that the Policy Model was one of the first, if not *the* first, strategic planning effort for businesses. Ansoff's (1965) book, *The New Corporate Strategy,* establishes strategic planning as a self-conscious enterprise. Long before strategic planning emerged as a dominant organizational paradigm, the history of strategic planning can be traced as far back as 400 B.C., with Tzu's (1983) *The Art of War.*

Bryson (1995) contends that strategic planning is "a disciplined effort to produce fundamental decisions and actions that shape and guide what an organization is, what it does, and why it does it" (pp. 4-5). Emphasizing similar points, Andrews (1987) defines strategic planning as "the study of the functions and responsibilities of the senior management in the company, the crucial problems that affect the success of the total enterprise, and the decisions that determine its future and produce the results desired" (p. viii). According to Moore (1995), strategy is a concept that "encourages the chief executives to see their organization in a wider, longer term, and more abstract context than is possible without its aid" (p. 65). Ukalkar (2000) suggests that "strategy" can be defined as a pattern of purposes and policies defining the company and its business. In all, a strategy is an underlying value system or common thread that joins the loosely coupled subsystems of an organization.

During the 1930s and 1940s, when the nation was emerging from the industrialization of many new industries, the dominant focus of strategic planning was on attempting to articulate the structures and processes conducive for organizational success, identifying the activities which were to be employed to ensure operational success, determining how resources were to be best utilized within constraints, and determining the expectations for organizational success at achieving its goals and objectives—including performance measurement and monitoring systems.

The focus of strategic planning during the 1950s and 1960s moved away from organizational policy and structure toward the management and promotion of growth (Ellram & Carr, 1994). Although there are a host of reasons for the growth of large organizations during this time, strategic planning can at least be credited with providing the vehicle for successful mergers and the growth of multinational conglomerates. Most large organizations had a strategic planning department and a strategic plan. These strategic planning "departments" spent inordinate amounts of time and resources establishing formal planning documents that extended to a number of volumes containing detailed plans that were so sophisticated that the architects of the plans could hardly follow them. Unfortunately, many of these documents where never fully understood by the key stakeholders nor the managers who had to implement many of the changes (suggesting a lack of strategic planning by the planning "committees") and, therefore, became SPOTS (Strategic Plans On The Shelf).

During the 1970s and 1980s, however, strategic planning fell out of favor as a mainstream, dominant organizational methodology. This is not to say that strategic planning was shelved and that organizations no longer considered planning a significant business activity. Most organizations were still actively involved in some form of strategic planning. What was more manifest during this period was the notion of quality management. It seems as though the whole customer focused total quality management movement determined that an organization needed a quality strategy, and only that. Strategic planning that considered a wider range of options was temporarily placed on the operational back burner.

Organizational efficiency and performance have been the dominant theme of the 1990s and early 2000s (Fung, 1999; Muther, 1998). Efficiency stresses the highest ratio of costs to benefits when developing and delivering public services. Strategic planning is concerned with delivering the right package of goods and services; the right levels of goods and services; the right attributes; the right costs; and all of this at the right time and price. Procurement officials will recognize this as the theme of the profession, which enforces the need for its involvement in strategic planning. As was discussed in Chapter 1, strategic planning goes to the very heart of an effective and efficient management system and, ultimately, the health of the community in which the government operates. Strategic planning is an organized effort to address community issues and problems for the future in a rapidly changing environment, within both strategic and operational constraints, and within both legal and administrative capabilities.

Strategic planning is an organized effort...

Effective strategic planning requires a lot of time and energy. The more an organization and its leaders are committed to planning, the more organizational resources will be utilized efficiently and effectively. Although increased planning means more cost, the cost incurred by the lack of proper planning may be even greater. There are always emergencies occurring which divert attention from the planning process in order to address the emergent issues that are not anticipated—perhaps a water main breaking and requiring significant resources to address the problem. There are very few, if any, jurisdictions in the United States that do not practice some form of crisis management. Many times, the crisis may occur as a result of lack of planning in the first place—perhaps a strategic plan that established an inventory of fixed assets, including the water lines, and noted their decay; or, as is most often the case, managers lack strategic direction and, therefore, choose the path of least resistance.

Strategic planning is about the future of the organization. When generating assumptions about a situation and anticipated future conditions, planners should always be cognizant that plans are, at best, an educated guess. Although decisions should be made with as much forethought as possible and with examination of all the potential benefits and consequences, planners must always remember that plans are simply views towards the future that can and will change. Therefore, it is difficult to plan, and strategic planning that integrates the sub-systems of an organization into a whole is even more difficult. It requires a tremendous amount of creativity and energy and a great deal of analytical capabilities and human relations skills. It is often very time-consuming and resource-intensive. Strategic planning is a critical part of the management responsibilities inherent in public life. Managers working in the public sector environment must always be aware of the political climate at any given time. Changes are always possible and occur at times without warning. Elected officials and chief administrative officers change, and so do many of the priorities associated with shifting demands of citizens. It is challenging to prepare meaningful long-range plans in the face of changing political agendas and shifting citizen sentiment. In many instances, these agendas only become public when elected officials are forced to articulate specific goals and objectives, which may only become apparent during the annual budget cycle; even these are masked through programmatic concerns.

The purpose of this chapter is to enlighten readers about the strategic planning process in government; to educate the reader about the various dimensions of strategic planning in the public sector; and to empower procurement professionals to embrace strategic planning as the key to organizational success and, ultimately, to the value added by procurement.

The Environment of Strategic Planning

*A*number of researchers have suggested that certain conditions must be present in order to effectuate strategic planning in the public sector (Quayle, 1998; Humpherys, 2001; Quayle & Quayle, 2000). A primary component is leadership. Clear, consistent, and visible involvement by elected officials, senior managers/executives, and service delivery managers is a necessary part of successful strategic planning and strategic management. In fact, all service delivery managers should be actively engaged in the formalization, implementation, and evaluation of the organization's planning process. Once leadership has taken an active role in strategic planning, a conceptual framework is needed to guide the strategic planning process. This strategic planning framework should stand as a beacon for all levels of the organization, one which supports the obtainment of goals and objectives as well as the collection and analysis of results. This framework is traditionally highlighted in a framework to organize, measure, and align the mission statement with the organizational goals and objectives. A uniform and well-understood structure setting forth how the strategic planning process works and a clear time line of activities for what is expected from each organizational sub-system should be clearly identified in the enabling framework.

All good strategic plans

identify what is needed

Effective internal and external communications must be established. Effective communication with service delivery managers, line and staff employees, elected officials, customers, and other stakeholders is crucial to successful strategic planning. It is the stakeholders of an organization who will ultimately judge how well the organization has achieved its goals and objectives—effectiveness. Service delivery managers who are entrusted with and expected to achieve strategic goals and objectives must fully comprehend how planning accomplishments are to be defined and what their role is in achieving that success. To capture these views, internal and external participants need to be a part of the development and deployment of strategic planning.

Process control and responsibility for outcomes must be clearly assigned and understood by all employees in the organization. All good strategic plans identify what is needed to accomplish specific objectives and to hold all managers and employees accountable for achieving organizational goals. Accountability, however, has various meanings and multiple dimensions within the public sphere. One means to ensure accountability is to establish an effective performance management system. In fact, without performance management and feedback, strategic planning cannot be successfully delivered.

Performance management systems must generate the necessary intelligence for decision makers. Typically, performance measures simply compile data without any reference to some articulated purpose. Therefore, performance measures must be identified which relate to specific goals and objectives, and these measures must provide timely, relevant, and accurate information for use in the decision-making process. Performance measures should be used to evaluate progress toward achieving the identified goals and objectives, and each measure should produce relevant information on the efficacy with which organizational resources are allocated. Further, each measure should show, in basic terms, how well each result compared to each identified intended outcome (strategy), as well as define how each measure impacted the efficacy of specific programmatic operations relative to specific strategic outcomes. The strategic plan should clearly articulate all performance measures that will be used to describe service delivery performance, operational direction, and established accomplishments, and then aggressively use these to improve the development and delivery of public goods and services for the stakeholders.

Performance measurement systems should, if possible, be linked to compensation, rewards, and recognition (Kaplan & Norton, 1992), although the utility of rewards as a motivator in strategic planning is still in question (Schreyog & Steinmann, 1987). In the private sector, successful plans relate individual performance evaluations and subsequent performance rewards to specific, identifiable measures of success; they relate financial and non-financial incentives directly to performance (Porter, 1997). By linking measures with rewards, employees are sent a clear message of what the organization sees as is important, but performance management systems should be based on objective measures that stress positive outcomes rather than a punitive stick approach to management. The most successful performance systems are not punitive systems; they are learning systems. These systems help an organization identify what works and what does not work in order to continue with and improve on what is working and fix or replace what is not working (Ruocco & Proctor, 1994).

As a measurement tool, performance indicators facilitate the evaluation of progress toward strategic goals and objectives (Rajagopal & Bernard, 1993). Results and accomplishments should be open and widely shared with an organization's stakeholders, including suppliers and elected officials. Information can be shared through various means, such as the Internet and intranet sites for real-time access. Other sources could be periodic reports (popular reports) or newsletters, public hearings, community presentations, articles in the newspaper, etc.

Limits to Strategic Planning in the Public Sector

*T*he literature has identified several limitations to strategic planning that must be discussed in order to effectuate successful planning. Procurement managers must be aware of and take action to overcome potential threats in order to effectuate successful strategic planning. According to Higgins (1991) some of the major challenges to planning are:

- lack of commitment to planning;
- failure to develop and implement sound strategies;

- lack of meaningful objectives or goals;
- failure to see planning as both a rational and creative process;
- excessive reliance on past experience;
- failure to identify the most critical factor for success;
- lack of clear delegation;
- lack of adequate control techniques and information on results; and
- resistance to change.

In addition to the potential problems with planning identified by Higgins (1991), other important factors have been identified which inhibit effective strategic planning. Environmental events cannot always be forecast or controlled. Events which are beyond the control of planning take place in the outside world. As stated previously, we cannot be sure of the future. Changes in technology and new processes are continually being developed that may have significant impacts on planning. Without the proper levels of participation and careful planning for implementation, organizational members may resist the proposed plans and objectives. At times, public organizations may even encounter the "Sacred Cow" situation, where programs or personnel may exist even though they are obsolete. In such cases, there may be limited support for the demise of these "Sacred Cows"; or, perhaps, these programs can be sunset. Outside consultants may play a vital role in bringing these circumstances to the appropriate people who can then take a fresh look at the situation.

The ultimate challenge to successful implementation of strategic planning in the public sector, as well as the private sector, is the coupling of the system with the various sub-systems. Many organizations fall victim to the belief that only a "corporate" strategic plan need be drafted; then, all the sub-systems will simply follow the chosen path to success. In most organizations, this is not the case. When managers are asked to fulfill the mission and are given latitude in determining the best means for achieving the goals and objectives identified at the organizational level, they are provided little guidance in how best to achieve the goals and objectives. When asked to change, most managers prefer to change as little as possible. This lack of communication has doomed many strategic plans.

A Strategic Planning Model

A number of strategic planning models already exist; and, even though there are differences between them, many tend to follow a similar pattern.

We claim no ownership to the development of the items identified in the literature. In fact, most authors proclaim the same basic elements when discussing strategic planning. Most of the strategic planning models examined include the following components:

- Evaluation of the current environment and, if applicable, evaluation of current strategy;
- Identification and evaluation of the role of the organization within its internal and external environments;
- Development/determination of anticipated adjustments to identified goals, objectives, and/or strategies;
- Examination and evaluation of practical alternative courses of action;
- Implementation of changes;
- Development of performance measures;
- Monitoring progress; and
- Evaluation and feedback.

The basic assumption is that by using or participating in implementing a series of decision sequences and analytical steps, an organization can determine the directions that its future strategy should follow.

The strategic planning model provided in Figure 2 in Chapter 1 must, at a minimum, include a mission statement, vision statement, goals, objectives, strategies (action plans), performance measures, monitoring processes, evaluation mechanisms, and feedback to ensure enhanced organizational effectiveness. Figure 2 represents an interpretation of the best models developed in the strategic planning literature based on an evaluation of each model's particular strengths and weaknesses. Although there is a significant number of competing models, given our extensive review of the literature, we find this framework most appealing.

Elements of Strategic Planning

*T*he **mission** of an organization identifies why it exists, what it is, and how it contributes to the local community within which it resides. The mission must describe the role of the entity as it relates to the jurisdiction as a whole. It must identify the common threads binding the organizational structure and its activities, and the mission must be articulated in such a way so that it can be clearly understood by the public. At a minimum, the mission should address the following questions:

- Who are we as an organization?
- Whom do we serve?
- What basic purposes do we serve, and why do we exist?
- What basic accomplishments are we established to accomplish?
- What is unique about our purpose/vision/mission?
- Is the mission/vision/purpose in harmony with the jurisdiction's enabling legislation?

A mission statement attempts to succinctly identify the purpose of the organization, distilling from enabling legislation or constitutional provisions the most important reasons for the organization's existence. The mission statement should be no more than **two or three** sentences in length. In many cases, there needs to be statements prior to the mission statement establishing context, and language after the statement defending positions identified in the statement. A mission statement reflects the essential purpose of the organization, particularly why it is in existence, the nature of the services provided, and the clients/customers it seeks to serve and satisfy. It is a current picture of the organization.

> *The mission must describe the role of the entity as it relates to the jurisdiction as a whole.*

MISSION STATEMENTS

Josephine County Government

We shall provide services in an open, honest and efficient manner.

We will encourage public involvement and co-operation to identify present and future needs and solutions.

We are dedicated to providing positive leadership and quality service.

The Village of La Grange Park

The Village of La Grange Park is committed to providing its citizens effective and efficient government services in a fiscally responsible manner. The village encourages cooperation among staff, Board, and other units of government in order to assess community needs and to determine the most effective manner in which to meet those needs. While committed to maintaining a professional and responsive atmosphere, the village must weigh individual needs against community standards and resources and determine what is in the best interests of all its citizens.

In contrast to the mission statement, a **vision statement** identifies where the organization wants to be in the future. It states the organization's uniqueness relative to its community, and it provides an image of the organization's future. Also, a vision statement identifies standards of behavior and the values that underlie the organization (what the organization believes in). The essential elements of the vision statement focus on those values to which the organization is committed and appropriate standards of behavior for all employees. Possible improvement paths, employee development programs, and measures or indicators of progress should be established for each element of the vision.

VISION STATEMENTS

Jackson County

Jackson County government shall strive to assure the provision of those services its constituents cannot provide themselves, to protect the public health, safety, welfare and environment for all without discrimination, efficiently and economically, to encourage economic development and to promote education in a safe and secure environment, with the end goal of creating the healthiest and most prosperous community in the nation.

Lambton County

Caring   Growing   Innovative

Goals identify what the organization is intending to accomplish and proposes the general ends toward which an organization directs its efforts. Goals are issue-oriented statements that reflect the priorities of the organization. Goals are statements about policy intentions and are generally ranked in terms of priority and resource commitment. Although goals stretch and challenge an organization, they must be realistic and achievable. The identification and articulation of **goals** is one of the most crucial steps in the strategic planning process. The goal development process begins to direct resources toward clearly defined purposes. Goals also identify where the organization desires to be in the future in obtaining the mission.

Goals should address the internal and external issues facing the organization, and each goal must be easily understood by the public. Although there is no agreed-upon number of goals for an organization, two to three goals per item identified in the mission statement are common and recommended. During goal development, the organization should begin identifying performance indicators that can be used to evaluate accomplishments. Goal formation should include, at a minimum, a high-level discussion and analysis of the following questions:

- Are the goals in harmony with the organization's mission and value statements?
- Will achievement of the goals fulfill or help fulfill the organization's mission?
- Are the goals derived from an internal/external environmental assessment, and do they reflect responses to stakeholder needs?

- Do the goals provide a clear direction for action?
- Are the goals unrestricted by time?
- Do they reflect organizational priorities?

STATEMENT OF GOALS AND OBJECTIVES

Ozaukee County Land Information Office

Goal 1: Integrate GIS into the daily activities of all departments that use spatial data.

The Ozaukee County Land Information Office will recommend changes in land record management that will facilitate:

- Improved data accuracy;
- Lower costs and increased efficiency on county government;
- Reduce duplication of effort between departments; and
- Provide improved access to information for users.

This goal will be achieved by the following objectives.

Objective 1A: In order to provide parcel level information, the county will produce a county-wide completed automated parcel database and spatial representation of parcels that are linked to each other and the assessment roll. Phasing will be by municipal number. Target completion date, January 2000.

Objective 1B: Ozaukee County's Environmental Health Department and Land Conservation Department need to extend the usability of both the topographic base mapping and the above mentioned automated parcel database. The county will begin integrating shoreland, floodplain and wetland zoning data obtained through the Southeastern Wisconsin Regional Planning Commission (SEWRPC) with the automated base map. Target completion date, January 2000.

Objective 1C: By the third quarter of 1999 the county plans to create and convert centerline data and information for all roads in the county. The county desires that road centerline data be integrated with census address ranges and parcel site addresses. Target completion date, June 2000.

Objective 1D: Develop land conservation applications for tracking conservation practices, non-point pollution control, and automated conservation planning tools. This process has started and will accelerate throughout 1999 with substantial progress by September 2000.

Objective 1E: Incorporate Pavement Surface Evaluation and Rating System (PASER) data into the road centerline data set. WISDOT is currently redesigning the local road database and the PASER program. The Land Information Office Coordinator will continue to participate in this redesign effort to forward the perspective of the county. This redesign is scheduled to be underway by 2001.

Objective 1F: Ozaukee County plans to participate in the regional year 2000 digital orthophotography project with SEWRPC. Although not formally organized, the Land Information Office has been requested to participate on a SEWRPC technical advisory committee. Target completion date, September 2000.

Objective 1G: In order to implement a comprehensive enhanced 911 system, the land information office will provide the necessary mapping data and assist in the evaluation of the existing software functionality. This review will include a recommendation to the Sheriff for any changes. Target completion date, June 1999.

Objective 1H: Assist the Construction Superintendent/Surveyor in the re-engineering of location based workflows in the Highway Department. Recommendation by June 1999.

Objective 1I: Establish a relationship within the Information Services Department on the creation of a point of contact for departmental GIS service assistance. Currently, the GIS has no presence within the IS department. Target Completion date, June 1999.

Objective 1J: Complete the topographic/planimetric base mapping of the entire county. Target completion date, December 2000.

Objective 1K: The Ozaukee County Land Information Office will manage on the county network infrastructure informational support for land records, GIS, and document imaging (ongoing task). Specific tasks include:

- Providing data linkage between the document imaging and the parcel maps;

- Continuing to support a network infrastructure that encourages communication and data sharing;
- Provide centralized and coordinated public access to data; and
- Leverage the use of the Internet/intranet for the dissemination of data.

A report on the above issues is to be completed by December each annual year.

Objectives are highly defined targets that require specific action. Objectives typically have shorter time frames than goals, and they may also identify specific performance indicators, such as quantity or quality criteria, in advance. All objectives must be achievable to some degree, measurable in terms of identified indicators, and establish timing and the direction, positive or negative relationships, of strategies. Specific goals can be divided into multiple objectives, and multiple strategies can be identified to achieve a given objective.

Although goals are typically broad statements of long-range intended purposes, objectives are much more specific in terms of accomplishments, quantifiable in terms of evaluation, and time sensitive. Objectives represent the extent to which goals will be achieved at the end of the time period for strategic planning purposes. Objectives should be derived directly from the identified goals, which imply a priority for resource allocation. Objectives must emphasize the results an organization is aiming to achieve and when they plan to achieve them. Objectives should clearly identify measures for specific results that the organization seeks to achieve during implementation of the strategic plan. These objectives should be easily understood by the public. The creation of objectives should, at a minimum, include an analysis of the following statements:

- Is the objective logically related to an identified goal?
- Does each objective describe an output or outcome in terms of identified targets, and are they time based?
- Is each objective realistic and attainable?
- Is the objective related to a specific foreseeable result or outcome instead of some internal process or output?

There is no limit to the number of objectives used in a plan. There must be at least one objective for each articulated goal. Objectives are exhibited in the strategic plan based on the assumed priority of each objective, beginning with those objectives which are determined to be of greatest importance relative to the goals that are weighted most important. Like their counterparts in goals, each objective should be no more than one or two sentences in length. Doran (1981) provides a conceptual framework for writing practical objectives. His method is called S.M.A.R.T.

Specific	Be specific in targeting an objective.
Measurable	Establish a measurable indicator(s) of progress.
Assignable	Make sure the objective is assigned to someone for completion.
Realistic	State what can realistically be achieved within budgeted time and resources.
Time-related	State when the objective can be achieved, that is, the duration.

Strategies are the identified methods to achieve specific goals and are used to carry out objectives. A strategy is the process or means for converting inputs (resources) into outputs (goods and services) and, ultimately, outcomes (the consequences of the outputs). All strategies must be sensitive to financial and other resource allocation decisions. Strategies are specific courses of action that will be undertaken by the organization to accomplish the articulated goals and objectives. While goals identify *what* the organization wants to achieve and objectives target *how* the goals are to be carried out, strategies identify the *methods* for achieving specific objectives. Rather than focusing primarily on process, good strategies focus on the necessary actions to accomplish objectives and provide the bedrock for performance measurement.

All strategies must be sensitive...

To develop strategies, the organization determines how best to achieve the results intended by the goals and objectives. Like objectives, there may be more than one strategy to accomplish each goal and objective. In identifying each strategy, associated cost estimates, potential benefits, and anticipated consequences of each alternative strategy must be evaluated. Strategies typically cross more than one program, activity, or functional area; therefore, one strategy may apply to more than one objective. In developing strategies, some of the major questions to consider include the following:

- If this strategy is implemented, is it directly (measurably) linked to a specific objective or goal?

- What are the projected benefits and costs of each strategy?
- Can each strategy be accomplished within legal and programmatic constraints? Is the strategy legal, and is it practical?
- Are there sufficient resources to implement this strategy (or strategies)?

Strategies must be easily understood by service delivery managers and line personnel and should be generally no more than one or two sentences in length. (In some cases, they may be rather long; it simply depends on the nature of the strategy.) Each strategy must highlight the methods required to achieve the objective. If a particular strategy is used to achieve more than one objective, or a particular strategy only accomplishes a portion of an objective, a matrix should be provided to show these relationships.

Performance Management is the development and alignment of performance objectives and the mechanisms for measuring the accomplishments of objectives to support the strategic goals and objectives of the organization. Petersen and Strachote (1991) contend that there are four types of performance measures:

- *Demand Measures* assess the severity of a problem or the scope of work to be performed.
- *Workload Measures* indicate the amount of work which must be performed to accomplish a specific task.
- *Efficiency Measures* compare resources used with results obtained. (Examples include ratio of procurement department operating expenses to dollar purchases and ratio of procurement personnel to total employees.)
- *Effectiveness Measures* determine how well a program or activity meets an objective or fulfills a need (e.g., inventory turnover rates, reduction in rush orders, development of new programs such as purchasing cards, cost of a purchase order).

Effectiveness measures are results oriented and are the most useful to decision makers in determining priorities for resource allocation decisions. Organizations normally utilize a variety of performance measures in order to monitor and assess current operations in the light of historical performance and establish future goals. As part of this process, it is useful to compare or "benchmark" the performance of a strategy against acknowledged, high performing leaders and against the general population of similar organizations. This allows comparisons of how the organization and its sub-systems are performing compared to others.

Up to this point, we have identified the basic components of the strategic planning process. Like most texts on the subject, the transition from the conceptual boundaries of strategic planning and how one goes about strategic planning in the public sector is waning. The remainder of this chapter is devoted to identifying the action steps necessary (but perhaps not sufficient) to develop and implement a strategic plan in the public sector.

An Action Agenda for Strategic Planning in the Public Sector[2]

Strategic planning is, at its most fundamental level, a process for determining **what** the organization wants to accomplish and **how** it will utilize its resources toward that end. All public sector strategic plans must be guided by legislative mandates and the specific needs of the public the organization serves. Figure 7 identifies the strategic planning action steps discussed in the previous chapter. Each of the steps will be discussed in more detail below in an attempt to present these two dimensions of strategic planning (what and how) in an action environment. The framework attempts to show a logical sequence for determining the exact location of the organization at any particular moment and can be used to evaluate emerging opportunities and threats before clarifying a set of objectives for which strategies can be evaluated, selected, and implemented. The framework can then be used in a sequential, and possibly iterative, way. Otherwise, the framework provides little strategic guidance. Like most planning processes, strategic planning follows a simple but time-consuming route. Strategic planning pertains to all areas of the public sector; and, in some cases, these analyses do not have to be formal and can be combined.

[2]Much of the information discussed in this section was adapted from the City of Grande Prairie, Alberta Canada, *Business Planning Framework* (www.city.grande-prairie,ab.ca/bp_frame.htm) and the Office of Planning and Budgeting, State of Georgia, *Guidelines for Strategic Planning* (www.opb.state.ga.us/op10001.htm).

1. Establish a preliminary Strategic Planning Team (internal). Identify key stakeholders and create a Strategic Planning Committee (internal and external).

2. Assess strengths, weaknesses, opportunities, and threats. This should be based on information from the internal and external environments and stakeholders analyses.

3. Draft a mission statement for the organization. Use concepts like provide quality service in efficient and effective ways to satisfy the community's needs. Values: safety and well-being of employees, promptness of responding to calls, training, and safety of public.

4. Identify and articulate goals and objectives, both long-term and short-term

5. Identify strategies to achieve goals and objectives, such as:

   • Assess merits of strategies.

   • Examine advantages and disadvantages of each strategy.

   • Select preferred strategies.

   • Eliminate options with little or no support.

   • Seek consensus on preferred option.

   • Identify implementation issues.

   • Identify resources—people, facilities, budget, organizational, and structural needs.

   • Build consensus on strategic decision.

   • Meet with key decision makers and other involved staff.

   • Meet with general personnel.

   • Announce plan to the public.

   • Develop an action plan (strategies).

6. Establish performance measurement systems. It is important to think in terms of how data can be gathered to evaluate goals and objectives.

7. Monitor progress and gather data, but data must be useful, reliable, and valid. Must have set-up established before data gathering begins—should think about data processing, how to store the data, who will take care of it, and which statistical programs will be employed. Bias should be eliminated. Some data may be "bad" but still useful.

8. Evaluate the plan and suggest changes based on evaluations.

Figure 7 - *Establishing strategic framework*

Source: Adapted from the City of Grande Prairie, Alberta, Canada, *Business Planning Framework*. Available from www.city.grande-prairie.ab.ca/bp_frame.htm.

Step 1. Establish a planning team and identify roles and responsibilities of key participants. The selection of team members has to be strategic in itself. Selecting internal and external participants is perhaps the single most important step in the process. If the participants do not know their responsibilities, are not committed to the planning process, and are unfamiliar with the organization, then the process is much more difficult to complete. Once complete, it is unlikely that substantial benefit will be gained. In cases where the participants do not have sufficient insight, the strategic planning process tends to lose focus. It tends to resemble a loosely coupled operating system.

Some of the tasks of the Preliminary Strategic Planning Committee consist of designing the process, establishing the time and resource constraints available for planning, establishing the desired process outcomes, deciding who will participate and how, and creating a structure for the planning process. The preparatory work is critical for the success of the process. By completing these tasks, a clear purpose and direction guide future endeavors during the implementation of the plan.

Determination of who should be on the original (as well as the ongoing) Strategic Planning Steering Committee (SPSC) should be determined through discussions with elected officials, key administrators, citizen groups, the business community, and, of course, the chief procurement official. From a limited number of discussions between these stakeholders, a list can be generated, and those same individuals should then be contacted to ensure that they are able and willing to participate. At this juncture, the roles and responsibilities of all concerned parties should be identified. This ensures that those involved in the strategic planning process understand what is expected of them, why it is expected, and who is to be involved. Figure 8 shows the potential key stakeholders in the public sector and can be used to start any strategic planning process. Appendix A provides a list of key stakeholders and suggests some potential roles each can play in the planning process. Remember, to some extent each of the stakeholders should participate on the strategic planning committee.

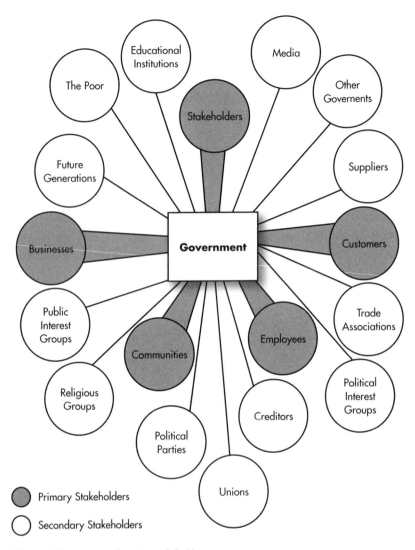

Figure 8 - *Strategic planning stakeholders.*

Organizational Stakeholders

Public sector planning literature uses the term "stakeholder." A "stakeholder" is considered any organization, group, or individual that can place a claim on the organization's resources or services or is affected by what the organization does or the services it provides. The Government Performance and Results Act (1993) at the federal level describes stakeholders as "organizations, groups, or outside managers with a vested interest in the efficiency of the operations or the success of the organization in delivering effective outputs and maintaining the viability of the program" (p. 23). Either definition underscores the reality that public agencies must respond to and are influenced by a variety of groups. The degree of influence varies, and the original planning committee needs to clearly understand these variances and adopt appropriate responses.

During the past decade, a growing interest in customer satisfaction has penetrated each sector of the economy. Public sector organizations have been motivated to more aggressively examine their role in meeting citizens' expectations. This motivation has prompted a preference among public organizations to use the term "customer." However, procurement managers are cautioned to exercise care and not exclude any group that may have significant influence on them, simply because it does not meet the strict definition of "customer." Overlooking such a group could prove to be a strategic error. All key groups that the organization should pay attention to must be represented.

To start, the committee generates a comprehensive list of both internal and external constituents and the relative importance of each constituent group. Next, the committee identifies the expectations that each has of the organization, the level of influence that the group has, and how well the organization is meeting the group's needs. Surveys, interviews, or focus groups are just some of the techniques the committee can use to find out what its stakeholders expect and how well the organization is meeting those expectations. Regular feedback from stakeholder groups is vital.

The committee should exercise care not to lose sight of the fact that its stakeholders are internal as well as external. The internal stakeholders are units or persons (employees) in the organization whose work depends upon another unit or person within the same unit. Recognition and understanding of the internal stakeholders and their demands on the organization play an important role in the organization's ability to effectively satisfy its external constituents.

At the department level, operation and management decisions about the process are needed. Frequently, a group, committee, or task force is designated to serve in this capacity. The team may be an existing group, the senior management team, some other type of management group, or a group specifically established for the planning process. While recommendations and suggestions may be made about the group's composition, a department head has final say about the participants and the group's structure within their respective areas.

Generally, the team's size and membership is consistent with the organization's scope and structure. The need to have adequate representation is balanced against the need to keep the group's size manageable. The strategic planning team decides the best way to carry out the planning process. The steps, while typically listed in a linear way, do not have to be followed in that order. It is possible to have two or more steps operate in parallel. The organization must keep in mind that strategic planning is cyclical, and its effectiveness flows from its repetitious nature. In addition to overseeing the planning process, the team may establish necessary workgroups; develop or review the mission, goals, and objectives; define the critical issues; develop a plan for managing those issues; and examine the implementation costs associated with the plan.

Step 2. Appraise the current situation and current strategy (SWOT analysis). Once all of the roles are identified, the next step is to ensure that the key stakeholders are informed about the various expectations in the strategic planning process. All documents at this juncture should be reviewed by the legislative body and feedback provided to individual/team members responsible for ensuring the development of the plan. Some of the most important questions are:

- Are we providing the right services?
- Are there service delivery areas we are not in but should be?
- Does the planning and budgeting process facilitate the attainment of legislative mandates?
- Does the process and the subsequent services meet citizen expectations?

SWOT Analysis. This is an internal analysis of the organization's Strengths and Weaknesses and the Opportunities and Threats the organization can potentially face. It identifies the service delivery areas the organization should be in, identifies service areas that should be sunset, assesses the economic and general conditions of the community, and evaluates the organizational and fiscal condition impacting the resource allocation process (Figure 9). It generates input from various stakeholders, such as citizens, identifies current issues impacting the organization, and measures how the organization has been doing in relation to stakeholder expectations. Combined, these steps define the starting point for the strategic plan. Some key areas the SWOT should address are:

- Management Personnel—their particular strengths and weaknesses;
- Political—council, commission, state level; support and threats across governments;
- Economic—tax structure limitations, user fees, future changes;
- Citizens—their needs, perceptions, expectations;

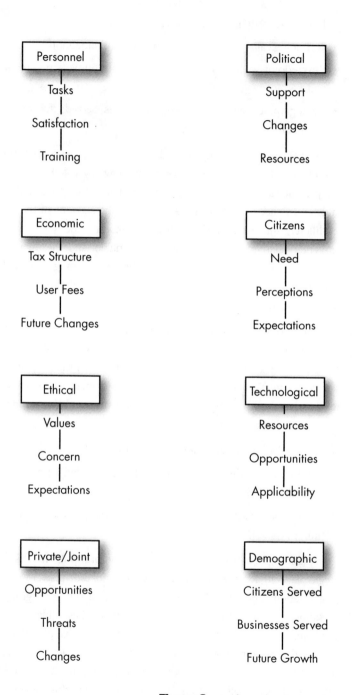

Figure 9 - *Analyses of environments.*

- Ethical—mostly internal values and standards;
- Technological—resources, opportunities and limitations;
- Private/Joint—what have others done, opportunities, and limitations; and
- Demographic—citizens served, businesses served, future growth potential.

Once the SWOT analysis is complete and the major issues and opportunities have been identified, the next step is to examine how key stakeholders impact the agency. A number of researchers contended that the goals and objectives (and the mission) of an organization must take account of the various needs of different interested parties who will represent some type of informal coalition. Their relative power will be a key variable; and the organization will, on occasion, "tradeoff" one against the other, establishing a hierarchy of relative importance. Some of the most common key stakeholders have been previously identified.

Step 3. Articulation of mission statement, vision, goals and objectives. This step consists of the articulation of the Mission, Vision, Values, Goals, and Objectives for the organization—the second phase of the planning cycle discussed in Chapter 1. Based on results of the SWOT analysis, the identification and articulation of the various goals and objectives should, at a minimum, address the following questions:

- Who and what are the priority and focus areas?
- Is there any additional service needed or deleted (functional and programmatic)?
- Are alternative service and budget level scenarios identified for planning purposes?

Ultimately, planning benefits from a broad collection of inputs. It is useful for the strategic planning team to obtain the perceptions of a diverse cross section of the organization. The individual vantage points of a variety of groups are likely to expose contrasting positions. The team notes these differences. The strategic planning team tends to assemble a comprehensive list of both accomplishments and areas for improvement by casting a wide net when seeking input. The team may want to devise a formal method for soliciting and compiling employees' ideas on both subjects. Another source of useful information is the data the agency has on performance. An agency may have several layers of information ranging from the very specific to more general. Part of the annual assessment should be a review of how well the agency met its performance targets for a given year. If the agency issues performance reports, then those should be examined.

The strategic planning team can use the compiled list of accomplishments as a starting point for discussion. The team may want to "brainstorm" to fill in any gaps that may exist. When the team has a comprehensive list, it should look at it and identify any patterns or groupings among accomplishments. The team should then discuss the significance of each group while considering the following:

- How does the accomplishment relate to the role and purpose that the department serves?
- Who benefits from each accomplishment?
- How does the individual/group benefit?
- What (if any) is the relationship of the accomplishment to the priorities identified in the plan?

After completing the analysis of the accomplishments, the group records the conclusions for use during the remainder of the planning process. The team then identifies areas for department improvement. One method to guide discussion is to have the group compare planned activities (from the previous planning period) with actual accomplishments. Any gaps in performance should establish benchmarks for areas that may need improvement. After describing an area for improvement, it is useful for the group to visualize how things would look if the process were improved. This mental construct is useful in showing the group how to overcome an internal weakness or turn it into a strength for the organization.

Departmental and Service Level Strategic Plans. These are the individual department's articulation of their specific vision, mission, and goals for implementing their portion of the strategic plan—objectives for accomplishing identified goals—and strategies for fulfilling objectives. The strategic plan identifies a comprehensive view of the organization's mission. However, converting this long-term vision into reality depends on a well-structured and coordinated effort in the short term. To successfully implement a strategic plan, each sub-system identifies the steps necessary to achieve stated objectives at the agency, division, section, work unit, and/or individual levels. While not especially difficult, only a coordinated effort translates organizational goals and objectives into specific

...identify any patterns or groupings...

short-term actions. Using an ongoing evaluation process, management monitors overall performance and provides remedial action where needed.

An action plan specifically outlines work tasks and activities for a designated period. A useful plan format shows the actions to be accomplished, indicates the responsible parties, provides a completion date, discusses the costs and resources needed for the action, and tracks actual progress. Before any organization commits to strategic planning, it must design a process to fit the purpose, and identify resources and the political environment that impacts the organization. The action plan provides a chance to resolve issues like the design of the process and the sequencing of its steps; resources available for planning; timing of the process; overall structure for the process; and participants and their roles.

When these activities are completed, each sub-unit has a draft work plan. Department management reviews the work plan, makes any changes, and agrees to it. After all the issues are resolved, the results are communicated to all concerned parties. Then, everyone knows the reasons for the planning process, how it is going to happen, the role that each person can play in developing the plan, and an expected completion date. The likelihood for success increases when service delivery managers and staff are kept fully informed and engaged in the process.

Depending on the size of the organization, one person or a team may complete the preliminary groundwork. Before beginning, the department head delivers a clear message to the employees that outlines the expectations for the work products, including:

- Activities or training to teach staff how to use planning and performance techniques;
- A communications plan to keep all employees fully informed about plan development and implementation;
- A time table for the planning process;
- A list of the planning steps, their expected duration, and the tasks for each step of the process;
- An organizational structure for carrying out the process; and
- An agreement on resource requirements.

Generally, public agencies are accustomed to a system that focuses mainly on inputs (money and people), process, compliance, and management control. Although it can be restrictive, personnel have grown comfortable with it. Successfully transforming an input-oriented planning process and performance process into a strategic system hinges on effective training. Personnel throughout the organization need to be trained on the philosophy behind a performance-driven culture and the benefits it offers. People must be shown how the system works and be given the tools that build their capability to use it.

A target-based or results-oriented management system is essential. To begin building this environment, offer a session(s) to agency personnel during the preplanning stage that describes the new process. What is going on and their role in the activity helps them feel a part of it. By promoting ownership, operational success becomes more likely. This is not the only possibility for training. Other training topics to consider are:

- Defining and measuring program, process, activity, or function results;
- Mapping and improving work processes;
- Individual's roles in agency outcomes; and
- Integration of strategic planning, budgeting, and performance measurement.

Another method to engage employees is to create a strategic planning resource center. Essential information and technical assistance should be in a place, such as a Web site, where every employee can access needed information. Everyone has access to these references. By creating and encouraging the use of a resource center, the organization suggests to employees that they are a welcome and valued part of the strategic planning process. In addition, it reinforces the notion that each employee plays a part in fulfilling the organization's mission.

A useful starting point in deciding where an organization wants to go is to discuss where it has been. This begins by examining the organization's recent accomplishments. A comparison of actual to planned achievements or actions adds another dimension to the dialogue. Discussions centering on how the accomplishments relate to the core business activities or purpose bring more clarity to the picture. This exercise provides an excellent opportunity for personnel to step back and reflect on what happened during the strategic plan's most recent implementation period. Staff analyze how well the strategic plan set the long-term direction for the organization. Particular attention should be directed to the degree that the hurry and strife of daily activities and periodic crises diverted attention away from the planned actions and identify the causes of this change.

Department managers and organizational leaders must seek to maintain a balanced discussion during this step. The organization can expect to have its share of accomplishments; but, by the same token, there will be some disappointments. As both achievements and areas for improvement are reviewed, management should foster a non-threatening atmosphere. A constructive, helpful discourse proves most productive. By telling service delivery managers and staff that disappointments are events that offer an opportunity for learning, management supports the move from a control culture to a strategic planning culture that does not punish risk-taking behavior, innovation, and creativity.

Step 4. Select the Preferred Strategies. During this step, individual priorities are articulated and approved, and each service level package is identified and funded within resource constraints. Drafting by departments of departmental service priorities without reference to available resources leads to many problems in the implementation stage that, in many cases, kills the strategic planning process. Described below are three methods for determining an order of priority for items within a group and may be used in combination with any other method that facilitates ranking of strategies.

> **Paired Comparison.** Simply stated, item A is compared to item B and is deemed to be of greater importance; Item A is then compared to Item C, and Item C is deemed to be of greater importance; Item A is compared to Items D, E, F, etc.; then, Item B is compared with Items C, D, E, F, etc., then, on to Item C, until all possible pairs have been considered. Then, tally how many times each item has been ranked the most important among the various pairings, followed by a ranking of the items based on highest to lowest frequency.

> **Colored Dots.** Another method is to write items on a sheet or a flip chart. Give three to five colored dots to each planning team member. Each color represents a numerical value (e.g., red has the value of five and represents the most important issue). Each person places the dots beside the items to be considered most important. The highest valued dot goes with the most important item, and the lesser values go with items of lesser importance. When all dots are placed, the resulting visual presentation will demonstrate which items are considered most important by the group as well as by individual participants. The scores are tabulated, and the selected items are listed in priority order.

> **"10-4" Technique.** Each member of the group receives 10 points to allocate. A member can give no more than 4 points to any specific issue. This effectively forces the participants to make hard choices about what is most important to them. Once members of the group finish allocating their points, the numbers are totaled. The issues are then ordered based on the number of points. The highest point total is the most important issue and so on. With each of the lists in priority

order, the team examines the lists of weaknesses, opportunities, and threats and determines which items should be designated for further consideration. This is to ensure that the number of issues is narrowed to be compatible with agency resource levels.

Based on findings of the method selected, and with input from departmental employees, ranking (high to low) of all programs, sub-programs, and activities can be conducted. To evaluate the impacts of delivery options within a planned service package includes analyzing the impact on:

- departmental or agency structures and personnel configurations;
- management processes;
- technology requirements, including information technology; and
- policy and legislative requirements.

Then, the preparation of the final service package for review can be accomplished. The packages should include:

- review (with possible revisions) and approval by Strategic Planning Committee;
- presentation to the Elected Officials by Strategic Planning Committee; and
- elected officials' review (with possible additional revisions), approval, and commitment to plan goals and objectives.

Step 5. Budget. A budget represents the allocation of resources consumed by each program and project, including capital and operating budgets, over a period of years. It also documents the final approval of legislation concerning approved temporal priorities, funding, levels of service, and standards of performance. Although most governments do not practice multi-year (three to five years) financial planning, the budget should, at a minimum, include:

- integration or cross-walk of operating and capital projects;
- identification and evaluation of performance measurements and performance outcomes included in budget documents;
- approval by elected officials;
- drafting of business plan processes by the Strategic Planning Committee; and
- identification of all amendments to the plan and completion of Individual Performance Plans, which link operational plans to performance measures.

Steps 6 and 7. Performance Review and Monitoring. In the delivery of programs and activities, performance monitoring and review are needed to ensure that the plan operations are being followed as stated (and to note where differences may occur). Each task accomplishment is to be evaluated and reported. Without linking review to some established metric, there is no way to assure that progress against the plan is measured and managed. Without such a review, there is also no way to isolate potential problems. The establishment of a process to monitor and evaluate operations establishes or isolates accountability structures and provides a means to judge progress of the plan against the plan. Within these domains, the quality, service, cost and time characteristics can be measured and judged relative to the plan's goals and objectives, including:

- monitoring and evaluating individual performance plans by program or activity;
- evaluations conducted by the Strategic Planning Committee of performance measures against departmental goals and objectives;
- review by Strategic Planning Committee of progress against the Strategic Plan;
- review and evaluation of changes to the plan that emphasize changes made or additions to the plan that have occurred through various management systems, including organizational learning;
- solicitation and evaluation of customer satisfaction results; and
- critique of individual performance measures and quality assurance standards that focus on outcomes.

Step 8. Evaluation and Feedback. Planning success depends on satisfactorily executing the plan and monitoring its results. A well-planned accountability system increases the likelihood of successful implementation (Figure 10). Accountability touches all levels of the organization. Service delivery managers, program managers, and employees are responsible for certain aspects of the plan. An accountability system reinforces that goals and objectives identified within the unit are evaluated, consistent with standard evaluation methods. Constructively using an accountability system generates interest in and builds commitment to the planning process.

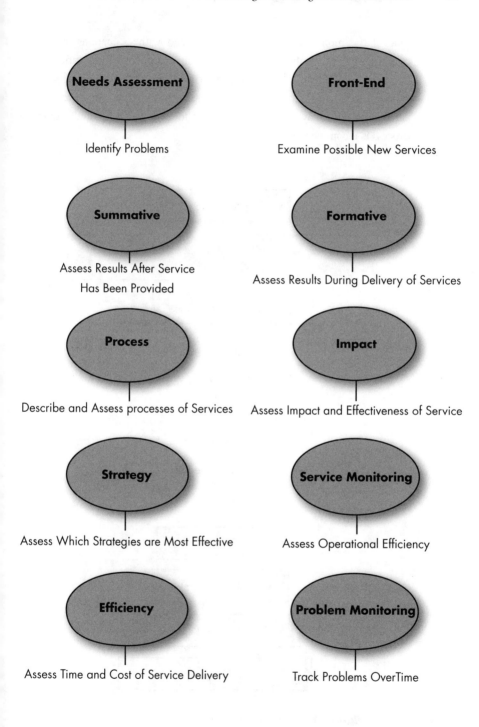

Needs Assessment
Identify Problems

Front-End
Examine Possible New Services

Summative
Assess Results After Service
Has Been Provided

Formative
Assess Results During Delivery of Services

Process
Describe and Assess processes of Services

Impact
Assess Impact and Effectiveness of Service

Strategy
Assess Which Strategies are Most Effective

Service Monitoring
Assess Operational Efficiency

Efficiency
Assess Time and Cost of Service Delivery

Problem Monitoring
Track Problems OverTime

Figure 10 - *Types of Evaluation*

One of the more difficult activities associated with evaluations is actually conducting the evaluation. Figure 11 provides a summary of the various steps necessary to conduct an evaluation in terms of strategic planning. Like most process charts, this figure provides the basics of conducting good evaluations. All steps may or may not be included, but following a logical and sequential process is recommended.

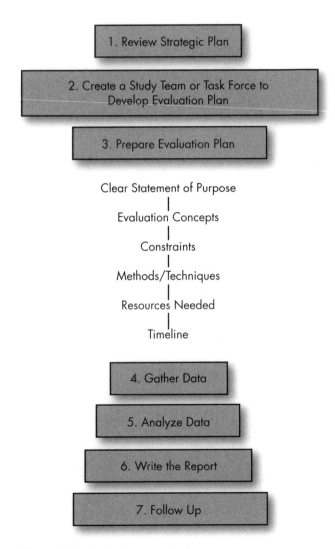

Figure 11 - *Conducting an evaluation.*

Conclusion

Strategic planning is a set of concepts, techniques and tools that help an organization assess where it is, decide where it wants to go, and determine the best way to get there. The strategic planning process is repeated periodically. A well-crafted strategic plan serves as an important management tool. It presents a wide-lens, long-term view of the organization's internal as well as external strengths, weaknesses, opportunities, and threats. It conveys agreed-upon priorities and provides an easily understandable, concise statement of strategic direction. It serves as a fundamental guide to evaluate all organizational resource allocation decisions and fosters cohesive program development.

For those who design the organization's process and collect information, an established format for the strategic plan is useful. While an organization may change the format of the strategic plan, the following elements are frequently included:

- mission statement;
- overview of the plan;
- expected benefits;
- recent successes;
- description of actual planning process followed;
- discussion of the plan's uses;
- summary of agency mandates;
- constituent analysis;
- description and priority of constituents;
- constituent expectations, now and in the future;
- objective assessment of how well constituent requirements are currently being met;
- core business activities;
- description of core business activities;
- discussion of priority of activities;
- situation assessment;
- external opportunities and threats;
- internal strengths and weaknesses;
- implications of opportunities, threats, strengths, and weaknesses for future operations;

- critical issues;
- description of the critical issues the agency faces and the challenges they present;
- explanation of priority assigned to the issues;
- strategic summary;
- goals the agency desires to pursue;
- objectives that describe specific outcomes sought;
- description of strategies and timetable to move agency in the preferred direction;
- assignment of responsibility for implementation of strategies;
- tracking and evaluation;
- process to monitor progress on plan;
- role of performance measures; and
- description of key performance measures.

The strategic plan prescribes a comprehensive view of the operations within an organization. However, converting this long-term picture into reality depends on well-executed efforts in the short term. To successfully implement a strategic plan, the steps necessary to achieve stated objectives at the departmental, division, section, work unit, and/or individual levels must be identified. While not especially difficult, only a coordinated effort translates department goals and objectives into specific short-term actions. Using an ongoing evaluation process, management monitors overall performance and provides remedial action where needed.

An action plan specifically outlines activities for a designated period. A useful plan format shows the actions to be accomplished, indicates the responsible parties, provides a targeted completion date, discusses the costs and resources needed for the action, and tracks actual progress. The linkage to strategic goals and objectives should be clear.

References

Andrews, K. R. (1971/1987). *The concept of corporate strategy.* Homewood, IL: Irwin, Inc.

Ansoff, I. H. (1965). *The new corporate strategy.* New York: John Wiley & sons, Inc.

Bryson, J. M. (1995). *Strategic planning for public and nonprofit organizations: A guide to strengthening and sustaining organizational achievement.* San Francisco: Jossey-Bass Publishers.

City of Grande Prairie, Alberta, Canada (1995). *Business planning framework.* Strategic and Business Planning, from www.city.grande-prairie.ab.ca/bp_frame.htm.

Demos, N., Chung, S., & Beck, S. (2001). *The new strategy and why it is new.* Booz-Allen & Hamilton, Inc., from www.boozallen.com.

Doran, G. T. (1981, November). There is a S.M.A.R.T. way to write management goals and objectives. *Management Review,* 35-36.

Ellman, I. M., & Carr, A. (1994, Spring). Strategic planning: a history and review of the literature. *International Journal of Purchasing and Materials Management,* 19-18.

Fung, P. (1999). Managing purchasing in a supply chain context—Evolution and revolution. *Logistics Information Management, 12,* 362-366.

Higgins, J. M. (1991). *The management challenge.* New York: Macmillan Publishing Company.

Humphreys, P. (2001). Designing a management development programme for procurement executives. *Journal of Management Development, 20,* 604-623.

Kaplan, R. S., & Norton, D. (1992, January-February). The balanced scorecard—Measures that drive performance. *Harvard Business Review,* 71-79.

McHugh, M. (1997). Trouble in paradise: Disintegrated strategic change within a government agency. *International Journal of Public Sector Management, 10*(6), 433-443.

Moore, M. H. (1995). *Creating public value: Strategic management in government.* Cambridge, MA: Harvard University Press.

Muther, R. (1998). Planning by design: Time tested and ready for the 21st century. *Advanced Management Journal, 63,* 33-39.

Petersen, J. E., & Strachota, D. R. (1991). *Local government finance: Concepts and practices.* Chicago: Government Finance Officers Association.

Porter, M. E. (1997). Creative advantage, *Executive Excellence, 14,* 17-18.

Quayle, M. (1998). The impact of strategic procurement in the UK government sector. *International Journal of Public Sector Management, 11,* 397-413.

Quayle M., & Quayle, S. (2000). The impact of strategic procurement in the UK further and higher education sectors. *The International Journal of Public Sector Management, 13*(3), 260-284.

Rajagopal, S., & Bernard, K. (1993, Fall). Strategic procurement and competitive advantage. *Journal of Purchasing and Material Management,* 13-20.

Ruocco, P., & Proctor, T. (1994). Strategic planning in practice: A creative approach. *Marketing Intelligence & Planning, 12*(9), 24-29.

Schreyög G., & Steinmann, H. (1987). Strategic control: A new perspective. *Academy of Management Review, 12*(1), pp. 91-103.

Spekman, R. E. (1989). A strategic approach to procurement planning. *Journal of Purchasing & Materials Management, 25,* 3-10.

State of Georgia, Office of Planning and Budget (2001). *Guidelines for strategic planning.* Available from www.opb.state.ga.us/op10001.htm.

Tzu, S. (1983). *The art of war* (J. Clavell, Ed.). New York: Delacorte Press.

Ukalkar, S. (2000). *Strategic procurement management for competitive advantage.* New Delhi, India: Oxford University Press.

CHAPTER 3

Strategic Procurement Planning (SP²)

*T*wo often cited axioms purported in the management literature are: "If you don't know where you are going, you will never know when you have arrived," and "a manager who has no time to plan has no time to live." Public sector service delivery managers beset by the press of day-to-day events often protest: "It is hard to devise a plan for draining the swamp when you are up to your fanny in alligators." We suggest in this chapter: "You should not go into the swamp without a contingency plan for alligators," and "if you want to go into the swamp, make sure you have enough supplies to survive, because we know there are hungry alligators in the swamp." In our view, the importance of strategic planning and, ultimately, the link between strategic planning and procurement planning cannot be overemphasized—Do not go into the swamp unless there is a specific need; and, if you go into the swamp, you had better hope the Buyer purchased the right alligator repellant.

Like strategic planning, good procurement planning requires a great deal of information acquired from many sources, both within the organization and outside the organization. The strategic plan should provide the corpus for developing procurement strategy and tactics. The procurement planning process is not overtly difficult, but it does require significant organization on the behalf of procurement professionals. This is especially true when other stakeholders are actively engaged in the planning process. Therefore, it is important that before the commencement of a planning initiative, you plan for planning. The time spent will pay dividends later. You will get back more than the time you invest up front.

The purpose of this chapter is to provide procurement professionals with the basic knowledge and techniques of procurement planning. It is almost redundant at this stage of procurement development to suggest that research has demonstrated that the financial benefits of developing integrated supply chain management, process redesign, and policy development may be far greater than the possible returns from a simple commodity or department cost/efficiency focus (Quayle, 1998).

Procurement Planning

Strategic Procurement Planning (SP^2) involves the transformation of the organizational mission, goals, and objectives into measurable activities to be used to plan, budget and manage the procurement function within the organization. According to Freeman and Cavinato (1990), procurement planning occurs across functional units and activities by extending the value chain/supply chain management concept to include procurement strategies. Strategies can, for example, aid in the development of supplier relationships to enhance the acquisition/production of goods and services consumed by the organization. It can help to identify specific functional demand attributes and/or link procurement spending to specific goals and objectives within the organization. Ultimately, though, the goal of SP^2 is to effectuate positive change in organizational culture, systems, and operational processes. This is accomplished by establishing a set of agreed-upon strategic and tactical goals and objectives within the operational context of the organization, thus linking resource allocation decisions in a priority-setting model. Informing managers to either confirm or change current procurement policy or program directions to meet those goals, as well as to share the results of strategic procurement goals and objectives with both internal and external procurement stakeholders, SP^2 seeks to generate an effective and efficient procurement system that:

- transforms a government's mission into valid and reliable outcomes that identify determinants of success within the procurement arena;
- shares these determinants with key stakeholders and the numerous customers and suppliers of government procurement processes and services;
- provides tools for assessing, managing, and improving the overall health and success of the procurement system;
- shifts from prescriptive, control-based procurement oversight to a continuous, forward-looking strategic partnership that involves service delivery units and suppliers; and

- identifies and includes the measures of service quality; cost (such as the cost of doing business); customer service, and employee integration/alignment, motivation, and skills to provide an in-depth, proactive procurement management system.

Not to minimize the importance of linking the organizational strategic plan to the procurement strategic plan, in some cases the organization may wish to avoid strategic planning. This does not preclude procurement professionals from actively planning themselves. The only disadvantage is that the procurement planning process could raise a number of substantive questions regarding the efficiency and effectiveness of current systems. This is a question that must be addressed by the Chief Procurement Officer. According to Frayer and Monczka (1997), some of the most common benefits associated with SP² are:

- It helps to focus attention on the organization's mission and link tactical procurement decisions to organizational strategy.
- It helps in designing future procurement strategy.
- It assists in designing or redesigning the structure of the procurement function.
- It allows procurement professionals to verify the legitimacy of procurement strategy consistent with the organization's strategy.
- It creates a framework for communicating with suppliers and cross-functional team members.
- It allows procurement resources to be assigned according to opportunities and risks.
- It gives a framework to review strategy implementation and control.
- It allows understanding the implications of cross functional problems and projects arising out of procurement decisions.
- It facilitates the identification of opportunities and threats for future procurement decisions.

The conceptual framework for accomplishing the procurement planning objectives identified above are provided in Figure 12. Remember, the initiation of all of the procurement activities to be accomplished in the short and intermediate term must originate from the organizational strategic plan. This is the source document by which all other activities are to commence. As indicated in the previous chapter, strategic planning is often conducted in a vacuum. One of the major reasons for the failure of strategic planning is the fact that the production of a planning document does not ensure the integration of strategic goals and objectives across functional boundaries. It is similar to the contention that producing a manual on safe driving guarantees safe drivers.

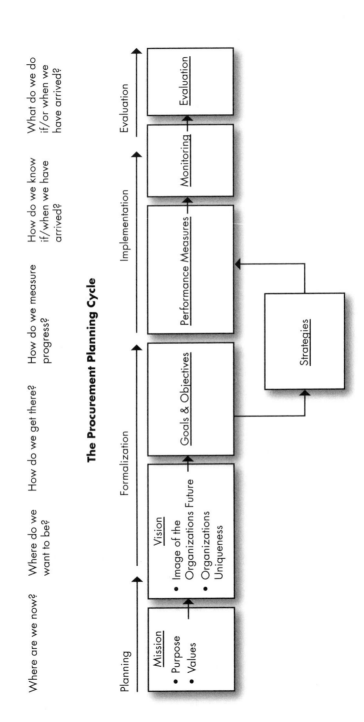

Figure 12 - *Strategic Procurement Planning Model.*

Procurement Model

*A*ll organizations consist of both vertical and horizontal functions that must share a common purpose, or the system fails to deliver the right goods and services to the consumer. Take, for instance, a recreation program that wants to provide a new swimming program for youths during the summer. Typically, the department would place a budget request next year to build the pool, and the following year they would anticipate staffing and maintaining the pool and subsequent programs. The budget office would examine the request, may even ask for additional information (such as projected usage), and make a recommendation on the issue. Then, it may be incorporated into the budget document or capital improvement plan; and the legislative body would vote on it, along with countless other requests.

Vertical and horizontal functions... share a common purpose

Under the SP² perspective, this process would be significantly altered. First of all, if the pool was not identified as a strategic issue, then the request would be halted by the budget office before it even got to this stage—unless there were noteworthy requests to have the pool added due to unforeseen or political reasons. The recreation department would have to present their case to the Strategic Planning Committee, at which time the committee would examine the costs and benefits of such a proposal. Given that the planning committee includes various stakeholders of government, there would be ample time to discuss the strengths and weaknesses of the proposal, explore relevant information regarding potential usage, examine alternative service delivery options, and compare various requests against each other to form more rational decisions. Once the pool is included in the strategic plan, the next step is to determine that all interlocking service areas are aligned in a cohesive manner. This is particularly true for procurement.

Procurement must take an active role in linking the loosely coupled operating environment of the organization. Other service areas, such as finance, budgeting, and human resource management, are secondary to the procurement function for a host of reasons. Many have contended that procurement is a "step-child" of the budget and finance function (see, for example, MacManus, 1992). Their argument is that all things purchased must be financed. In this capacity, they are correct; but procurement is much broader than simply assigning costs to goods and services consumed in an organization and establishing compliance-based audit trails. Procurement involves the management of resources to effectuate the determination of the right product, at the right time, and at the right price to organizational consumers.

Developing an Organizational Level Procurement Plan

*A*s stated earlier, the procurement function is the entire process by which all classes of resources (human, material, facilities, and services) are obtained and includes such items as procurement planning and strategy development, specification and standards development, commodity research, selection of suppliers, negotiation, contract management, disposals, supplier performance monitoring, relationship management, and inventory management. Not only must the procurement function effectuate these activities, it must be accomplished within the confines of the strategic planning process.

The origination of the procurement planning process must include introspection—the examination of procurement's ability to achieve the organizational strategic goals and objectives. If there is a potential mismatch, procedures must be in place to rectify the situation. The primary dimensions of this introspection are the examination of the administrative arrangements for the procurement function, the identification of the procurement systems and processes, and the identification and placement of skilled procurement personnel at key decision points along the procurement process (Rink & Fox, 1999). Evaluating procurement's ability to deliver the strategic procurement focus capable of supporting the strategic plan requires that annual evaluations be conducted to ensure that administrative arrangements for the procurement function are in place, that the purchasing systems and processes are fully understood by all parties concerned, and that procurement has the capability to rectify situations when needed.

The SP² Process

*L*ike the strategic planning process discussed in the previous chapter, the strategic procurement planning process should originate with a small planning team. Given the broad nature of procurement, the planning team should be made up of one to two procurement personnel, one to two department personnel, one to two suppliers, and one person from the finance area. The task of the organizing committee should be to develop the mission, goals, and objectives; identify participants to include on the SP² team; and establish general guidelines and timetables for the SP² process. They should also be actively involved in the first couple of meetings with the SP² team to ensure that they are heading in the right direction. The original planning team may even be included in the SP² team. This is a judgment that must be made by the procurement professional spearheading the initiative.

One method to help identify the preliminary mission of the procurement department is brainstorming. Brainstorming is a semi-structured, yet free-wheeling, creative dialogue involving a high degree of give-and-take among team members. Ideas are suggested, placed for everyone to see, and no ideas during the early stages are discouraged. In fact, team members build upon the ideas and suggestions of each other. The range of possibilities is limited only by the group's creativity. The dynamics associated with brainstorming can lead to an overall better articulation of the various components of the SP². Finding viable solutions or responses to critical issues takes a thorough understanding of the issue, the challenges it presents to the procurement agency, and the advantages and disadvantages of the alternatives. While the planning team examines each alternative, it should look for any potential barriers to implementing the strategy. A healthy debate about the effort required to minimize or eliminate a specific weakness can possibly uncover likely implementation problems. This gives the procurement agency the chance to decide if it wants to address the weakness or to abandon that alternative. Awareness of the realities before committing to action can save the agency a great deal of time, resources, and frustration. After exploring its options, the team drafts the mission statement and vision statement to include in the agency's strategic plan.

PROCUREMENT MISSION STATEMENTS

Virginia Commonwealth University

The Department of Procurement and Payment is a service organization whose function is to support the teaching, research, and public service mission of Virginia Commonwealth University. Support is provided by ensuring the entire procurement cycle (involving purchase and payment activities) is performed in a manner that demonstrates our continuous dedication to providing excellent customer service; effectively satisfies the needs of the end-user; promotes positive vendor relations through diversity in expenditures and timely payment of invoices; develops and fosters business relationships with small, minority, and women-owned businesses; achieves cost savings through effective use of procurement methodologies/principles and streamlining administrative operations; and seeks more efficient and innovative ways to conduct public administrative activities, while complying with all laws of the Commonwealth of Virginia.

The Health and Hospital Cooperation of Marion County

The mission of the Purchasing Department is to responsively and efficiently manage the procurement of supplies and services for the Health and Hospital Corporation while maintaining the highest level of professional ethics and integrity.

The Purchasing Department will manage the procurement process in order to acquire quality supplies and services at the lowest price; give timely and effective support to ensure that the requirements of the corporation's services to the community are met; provide potential suppliers with equal consideration of their products and services; and instill public confidence that contracts are awarded in an equitable and economical manner.

The Purchasing Department will continue to offer courteous and dedicated assistance to all of its internal and external customers.

Another effective method for identifying and seeking preliminary approval of the mission of the procurement department is to survey all key stakeholder groups. Given that a number of procurement organizations are familiar with customer surveys, the adoption of this method of data collection is relatively simple. Key stakeholders can be surveyed to help identify the procurement departments SWOT. In addition, a draft mission statement, along with some goals and objectives can be sent to elicit response.

There are several options for developing goals and objectives within the procurement function. Given that the preliminary planning team has developed rough mission, vision, goals and objectives, the SP² planning team can act as a single group, create subgroups of the team, or establish a new team all together to look at certain critical issues. One means for identifying which of the three options is best should be based on the number and magnitude of the issues affecting the procurement process. To make effective use of a team member's time, it generally works best to create small workgroups and assign each group one or two issues. The final goal statements are distributed to the appropriate groups for review and critique. For those instances when the organization has adopted a formal strategic plan, the organizational goals establish the strategic direction at the department level. These goals must focus procurement's actions in a clearly defined way, or the system becomes uncoupled. The department goals and objectives must be detailed enough to facilitate specific action, but not so specific that the goals and objectives inhibit innovation and creativity at the operational level. They should not be simply a recasting of the procurement agency's mission, nor should they reflect "business as usual."

In developing procurement goals and objectives, team members must think about issues and how things might be done differently, if the agency managed it more effectively. The SP² team should focus on the end state, not the process. During this step, team members should not get bogged down with identifying solutions, barriers, and problems. Each member should try to identify specific criteria of success and capture the model in written form. In some instances, members may actually want to draw a picture to illustrate their conceptual model. Visual expressions should not be discouraged, because this mode of communication tends to spark additional ideas or trigger other team members' creative capacity.

The team should identify anything that could prevent or hinder the implementation of an alternative. The objective is to identify foreseeable problems early on. Because removing barriers can be costly, anticipating them and estimating their costs is an important variable when deciding which option to implement. Refining possible alternatives into useful goals and objectives draws heavily on the experience and expertise of group members. Members with specific knowledge or expertise regarding a specific issue can describe broad, long-term means for achieving a goal. The primary components or features of the alternative should include items such as intended results or outcomes, implementation timetable, groups and persons responsible for implementation, and required resources. Before the strategic planning team reviews alternative options, it should also develop criteria to assess them. The team leader briefs the members on the criteria's intent and how to use it. Following is a list of typical factors to use to decide among options:

- Does the option make sense in light of likely trends, the agency's mission and vision, and anticipated organizational change?

- Is the option based on realistic assumptions?

- Does the procurement department have or can it acquire the skills, resources, and commitment required to pursue a given option?

- Is the option consistent?

- What are the risks of implementing this option?

- What contingency plans have you identified?

- When must the department act, and when will it receive tangible benefits from pursuit of an option?

- Does the option significantly limit or enhance the procurement department's flexibility to fulfill its mission and achieve its vision?

- Can the procurement department realistically implement the option?

The SP^2 planning team evaluates the alternatives developed to manage each critical issue. Once the groups have had sufficient time to examine the specific issues, all members should share their ideas in a group meeting. A facilitator should be present (other than a member of the team) to record ideas and ensure that everyone has an opportunity to discuss the given issues. The planning team looks at the responses, identifies themes or similarities, and talks about differences. The team then synthesizes the answers into coherent goal statements to which everyone can agree. When the team establishes the goal statements, it should remember:

- Goal statements should be challenging, yet realistic in terms of what the department reasonably expects to accomplish.

- Goals address priorities and the results of the internal/external assessment by advising management of critical issues.

- Goals collectively should provide enough detail to guide operating decisions, yet be flexible enough to generate creativity and innovation.

- Goals should not conflict with one another.

- Goals should be written in clear, simple language, which can be easily understood by all department employees as well as the general public.

- Goal statements should be brief and to the point. One or two sentences are generally adequate. In some cases, the department may need longer goal statements, but short direct ones are usually best.

GOALS AND OBJECTIVES

Salt Lake County, Department of Contracts and Procurement

GOALS

Contracts & Procurement management recognizes certain responsibilities. To achieve these obligations, our goals include:

- Pursuing professional excellence and communicating this to using agencies, administrators, officials and the public.

- Striving to improve employee motivation and productivity.

- Controlling the costs of the purchasing operation.

- Working with using agencies and with vendors to bring about cost reductions.

- Developing a continuing program for staff and supervisory training.

OBJECTIVES

Creation of this division represents recognition of procurement as a centralized activity. In order to make an effective contribution to the county of which we are a part, must be attuned to and oriented toward the overall objectives of the organization. Centralized purchasing objective is to achieve savings through the application of efficient management techniques, especially through volume buying. Savings may accrue by combining volume purchases, proper planning and coordination, and improved specification and standardization.

Each member can receive a copy of the list, or it can be enlarged to poster-size and tacked on the wall. The group may use any or all of the following questions to facilitate the development of goals and objectives:

- Does the goal/objective address critical issues confronting the department?
- Does the goal/objective chart a clear course for the department?
- Is the goal/objective consistent with the department's mission and mandates, and does it require any further guidance from leadership in the executive branch?
- Does the goal/objective reflect the core business activities and strategic direction for the department?
- Is the goal/objective realistic, achievable, and challenging?

Analyzing Options–Generating a Procurement Profile[3]

A starting point in the development of a sustainable procurement plan that can enhance the effectiveness of the SP^2 process is to extrapolate all procurement expenditures for every department for a specific period of time. Typically, this is produced for a five-year period. The collection and synthesis of this information should be used to generate a procurement profile. The profile will provide baseline information that will allow the planning team to evaluate where the organization is spending its resources. The next phase is to evaluate each supply market and associated levels of risk for each expenditure category. Following these two phases, each supply market from which the government has purchased specific goods and services should be evaluated.

The procurement profile can then be used to determine the impact of the expenditure patterns on the various supply markets that provide goods and services to the organization. Finally, historical and current supply patterns can be forecast to estimate both the intermediate and long-term procure

---

[3]Much of the text used in this section was reproduced, with permission, from the *Corporate Purchasing Guide* produced by the Queensland State Government, Department of Public Works, Queensland Purchasing Division (February, 2001). The Web site and documents produced by the Queensland Purchasing Division provide a rich array of source information that can assist state and local governments in developing their own procurement strategy, as well as various documents to facilitate a better understanding of the relationship between organizational strategy and procurement strategy. You can visit the Web site at http://www.qgm.qld.gov.au.

ment needs of the organization. These estimates provide useful benchmarks for establishing and evaluating the effectiveness of the procurement plan, the nature and risk associated with various supply categories, and the nature and timing of resource demands.

In order to develop this level of sophistication, a coordinated effort must be initiated between procurement and the individual agencies within the organization to gather information on the procurement spend, supply risk, market segmentation, procurement integration, and procurement forecast (Figure 13). Each of the components of the procurement process will be discussed below.

A first step in accumulating the information to generate a procurement profile is to identify the various agencies of the organization. In most cases, this can be an easy task by simply reviewing the organizational chart. The organizational chart will offer enough detail to provide the lay reader with the various agencies involved in the procurement function. Once all the agencies are identified, the next step should be the identification of all programs/activities associated with each agency. This may require further analysis and discussions with the various agencies to identify what is being accomplished, how it is being accomplished, and who is involved in accomplishing the task.

Next, the general and accounts payable ledgers of the organization should be examined. These documents are a good place to start, given that they typically provide a rich source of information regarding the quantity of items purchased, when the item was purchased, who purchased the item, from whom, as well as other general vendor information. Utilizing the information contained in the general and accounts payable ledgers (as well as all supporting documentation) requires working with finance or accounting personnel to obtain expenditure reports for all of the goods and services the organization consumed. A breakdown by general ledger account code usually provides sufficient detail to commence this process. Unfortunately, unless the procurement department has maintained this information, the general ledger codes are not a good descriptor of the goods and services charged to a particular code. It may be necessary to "drill down" into the general ledger codes and categorize the transactions into meaningful groups for generating the procurement profile. A suggested criterion for establishing the benchmark for grouping purchases is that groups represent related goods and/or services that might logically be purchased together in the same purchasing action and from the same market sector. For example, in some organizations, RFPs may be invited for facilities management as one product group rather than a number of separate items, such as cleaning, security services, air conditioning, etc.

Procurement Spending Patterns. This information will form the basis for what is commonly referred to as a procurement profile. A procurement profile will contain, at a minimum, responses to the following:

- What goods and services are purchased?
- Which department is buying specific goods and services?
- How much is spent on each good and service?
- How are goods and services purchased? *— inhouse or outside*
- From whom are the goods and services purchased?
- What is the geographical location of suppliers?

Supply Risk. Determine the level of risk associated with each category of item purchased. Goods and services can then be categorized by their relative expenditure and difficulty of securing supply, of which risk is a factor. The tool commonly used for this categorization is supply positioning.

- How critical are the goods and services to the organization?
- What is the risk associated with each good or service purchased based on:
  - product-related risk;
  - organization-related risk;
  - supplier-related risk; and
  - market-related risk?
- What are the key supply markets from which the organization spends?
- How many suppliers are there, and what are their market shares?
- What is the availability of alternative or substitute products?
- What is the degree and type of competition between suppliers?
- What is the nature and quality of the supply chain?
- What environmental factors affect the supply market?

Market Segmentation. Examine the impact of the organization's purchasing activities on its key supply markets.

- What is the organization's value as a customer?
- How are suppliers likely to view the organization's business?

Procurement Integration. Assess each department's procurement function, including its structure and role, systems processes, and capability.

Procurement Forecast. Determine both the intermediate and long-term purchasing needs of the organization, and develop strategies to facilitate the goals and objectives of the procurement plan and the organizational strategic plan.

Figure 13 - *Components of procurement planning.*

Source: Adapted from the Corporate Procurement Planning, Queensland State Government, Department of Public Works, Queensland Purchasing Division (February, 2001).

The NIGP provides a very useful Commodity/Service Code book for public sector procurement agencies. The Code is maintained and supported by Periscope, a technology company focused on the public sector and the sole custodian and marketer of the Code under an ongoing agreement with NIGP. The Code is the most widely used commodity/services code in the public sector and is utilized by more than 1,400 governmental entities, including 33 states. Ohio and South Carolina, along with the California University system, further affirm the Code as the standard tool for government purchasing at every level and location of the public sector.

In addition to reviewing the accounts payable, general ledger, and the NIGP Code, information can be gathered from vendor listing files; departmental staff who engage the suppliers; and general references, such as the Internet or Yellow Pages, can help identify the market(s) in which the suppliers are operating, in addition to the suppliers themselves. In some instances, the same supplier may appear under different categories. For example, an office supply company may appear under office supplies, computer equipment, and furniture. Therefore, sub-categorization that cross-lists vendors and product or service types may be useful to provide more detail to a larger category and to relate different groups to specific commodities or services.

Some of the preliminary factors to consider when categorizing expenditures include the difference/similarity in risk involved with procuring the various goods or services, supplier capability, application of the product or service in the department/agency, and similar or related markets. Nails, hammers, nuts, and bolts may be categorized into "building hardware" for an agency under-taking building maintenance. For each item, the purchase risk is similar—low risk with supply widely available and the items put to the same general use. In the case of consultancy services for engineering and architectural services, these would be separated. The purposes of the consultancies are sufficiently different to warrant division at this juncture in developing the profile, given that supplier capability required for building engineering and design is quite different; and the levels of risk in each instance may also vary. Remember, it is always easier to separate spend categories in the beginning. They can always be aggregated later.

All procurement spending information should be placed in an electronic database for easy reference and analysis. Expenditures can then be ranked from highest to lowest to ensure that high expenditure areas are categorized first— typically, the top 20% of entries account for approximately 80% of the total procurement spending. It may be appropriate to categorize the other entries according to the NIGP Commodity/Service Code under which they appear.

By focusing effort on the top 20% of the highest expenditures, the likelihood to transform the procurement profile increases to an intelligence-gathering device for strategic planning.

Once the expenditure profile is generated, the next step is to discuss the outcomes of the categorization with the key stakeholders involved in purchasing or supplier management to ensure that the goods and services are logically grouped in relation to the use of the products. All goods and services should be included in the profile regardless of who purchases the goods or services or how little or how much is spent on a particular item. Many agencies delegate purchasing authority to various functional areas, and there may be an inclination to exclude such expenditures. This is particularly true in service areas, such as public safety or public works. Also, internal transfers and inter-departmental transfers must be identified because they can distort the information extracted from accounts payable. Remove these if necessary to get an accurate picture of the procurement expenditure. Also, remove salaries and salary-related costs, as well as differentiate between funds for procurement purposes; but, remember, if the organization has a fully articulated activity-based costing system in place, then personnel costs and other associated costs (such as overhead) can be determined for each spend category.

Once a procurement profile is generated by item, by department, and by fund, past expenditures can be extrapolated and analyzed using vendor-related information. The vendor profile should include, at a minimum, the following:

- vendor name and identification number;
- vendor address and zip code (to be used in a regional analysis);
- the total amount spent with this vendor for the fiscal year;
- the number of invoices processed for the vendor, the amounts and transaction method (RFPs, procurement cards, emergency purchase orders, etc.);
- the general ledger codes to which the expenditure was posted for the vendor; and
- which department/agency used this vendor (with amount, if possible).

Vendor identification numbers can be used to determine the amount spent on each item for a particular supplier or group of suppliers for a particular time frame. Collecting zip code information can be used to determine local and regional spending patterns. The invoicing technique can be used to determine if the government may be overly reliant on one particular solicitation technique. This information can also be used to determine if invoices to a particular vendor can be consolidated in order to decrease transaction costs. Tracking which agency uses a particular vendor can provide valuable information for planning purposes.

Supply Positioning

*M*cHugh (1997) suggests that there are two major forces impacting the nature of government procurement: (1) the difficulty of securing a supply of goods and services and (2) the amount expended for each good and service consumed by the organization. Using a procurement management technique termed "supply positioning," goods and services can be plotted according to their relative difficulty in securing supplies and the amount expended. This is a good way to determine where the procurement effort should be focused in the procurement plan for the future. Figure 14 shows how a typical supply-positioning chart appears. For most governments, the lower left-hand corner shows the major concentration of goods and services. This is a reflection of the Pareto principle, where 80% of the items procured account for only 20% of procurement spending. The majority of these items are usually available from competitive markets and represent little or no risk.

As Figure 14 suggests, there seems to be a strong positive correlation between expenditure and difficulty of securing supplies identified on the supply-positioning chart. Generally, the greater the expenditure on particular goods and services the greater the difficulty in securing supplies. The relationship between amount and risk in the supply market and the costs associated with a product are not perfect, so a low-cost item may represent a high degree of difficulty in securing supply or a high cost item may pose no significant risk for the department/agency. One of the key determinants of the successful utilization of the supply-positioning chart is to ensure that complex categories of products are separated to the lowest common denominator. For example, purchases labeled "information technology" can be split into a number of markets, including information technology consultancies, personal computers, computer peripherals, and software and computing contracting. This is important because each market has different characteristics, and the risks of securing each may be different.

The importance placed on particular goods and services will depend on whether it is critical to the goals and objectives identified in the strategic and procurement plans. For example, if the supply of gasoline or bulletproof vests was disrupted, a police department would be exposed to greater risk than a

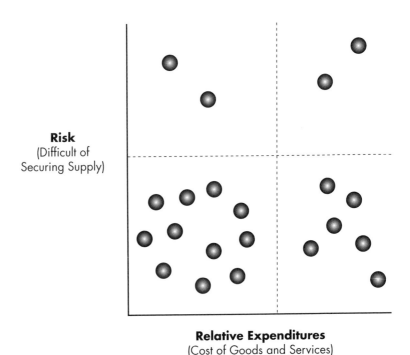

Risk
(Difficult of
Securing Supply)

Relative Expenditures
(Cost of Goods and Services)

Figure 14 - *Supply positioning scatter plot.*

recreation department or administrative support functions. The level of risk associated with a product or service will also depend on the probability of supply failure—the chance the product will not be available at the right time, right place, and in the required quantity. In some cases, even though the impact of the risk may appear to be high, if the probability of the risk arising is low, then the overall risk rating for that product or service will be low. For example, while it is critical for police to have high quality failsafe equipment and supplies, the markets for these products are generally reliable and product standards high. Departments are also vulnerable if or when a supply market is unreliable or uncompetitive. If the department requires a specialized product that is only available from one supplier, it is highly exposed to potential problems with the performance of that supplier. On the other hand, if that product were available as an "off the shelf" item from a number of suppliers, the level of risk would be lower.

When estimating the level of supply risk, risk exposures arise from a variety of sources. For example, risk may come from the purchasing organization, the product or service, the supplier, and/or the commodity market. These risks are to be considered simultaneously in assessing the overall difficulty of securing supplies. To determine the extent to which a competitive supply market exists, market research into the following areas is suggested:

- the type and number of suppliers within a market;
- an estimation of each supplier's market share;
- the availability of alternative or substitute products or services;
- the level and nature of competition within supply communities;
- the department's value as a customer to the supplier; and
- environmental factors affecting the supply market.

Supply market research essentially means getting to know how the market works, the direction in which it is heading, who the key stakeholders are, and the value they place on a government's spending. A more robust discussion of conducting market research is provided in Chapter 5. Without this information, it is not possible to accurately assess the risks (difficulty of securing supplies) associated with different purchases or to develop effective procurement strategies.

Once the risks of supply are identified and a reasonable estimate is provided regarding risk factors, the supply-positioning chart can be segmented for planning purposes. As Figure 15 shows, the goods and services in the easy-to-secure supply (low degree of difficulty to secure supply) and low-relative-expenditure category will demand substantially less attention than goods and services in the other categories. Goods and services in the high-expenditure and high-risk quadrants require different planning needs. A supply-positioning chart is a decision-making tool that can be used to locate expenditures relative to some metric and help procurement professionals determine appropriate strategies for satisfying the organization's procurement needs.

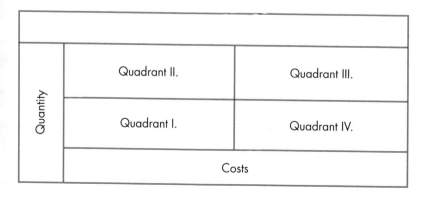

Figure 15 - *Supply positioning chart.*

As a guide, the four major procurement categories are:

Q I: Goods and services with a low degree of difficulty of securing supply and a low expenditure relative to total procurement spend. These items collectively make up a relatively small proportion of the total expenditure on purchased items.

QII: Goods and services with a low degree of difficulty of securing supply and a high expenditure relative to total procurement spend. These items collectively make up about a quarter of the total expenditure on purchased items.

QIII: Goods and services with a high degree of difficulty of securing supply and a low expenditure relative to total procurement spend. These items collectively make up a very small proportion of the total expenditure on purchased items.

QIV: Goods and services with a high degree of difficulty of securing supply and a high expenditure relative to total procurement spend. These items collectively make up over half of the expenditure on purchased items.

General procurement objectives can then be developed based on where goods and services are located on the supply-positioning matrix. Although there is some arbitrariness associated with this graphical depiction of the supply continuum for the organization (such as where to draw the dividing lines), the ability to pictorially represent the potential procurement strategies for each quadrant provides some simplicity to an otherwise complex issue.

Assessing Procurement's Impact on its Key Supply Markets

Assessing the impact of the government's purchasing activities on its key markets is essential to gaining an understanding of its potential influence in a market and the associated risk factors. Is the organization in a position to negotiate change in the market, and would suppliers be willing to change/improve performance to meet the needs of the government? Supply market research allows the government to gauge its significance as a purchaser by considering:

- their market share as a customer;
- whether they are easy or difficult to deal with as a customer;
- who the major customers are in the market and whether the government competes with them for the supplier's attention;

- whether there are opportunities for alliances with other public sector buyers; and

- whether the government is an avenue for suppliers to access other customers.

A number of businesses today also evaluate their client's worth in order to determine the amount of effort they wish to exert to maintain the account. Suppliers will assess the total costs of doing business with the government in order to determine if it is a profitable account. A procurement management tool called "supplier preferencing" can assist in determining how suppliers may view government's business.

The supplier will look at the dollar value of the account and then classify the attractiveness of the account. The account may be viewed in four general categories. If the government is viewed as a nuisance account, the supplier may show little interest in the government's business. The objectives for both parties should be to reduce transaction costs and risks; and, in some cases, the government may wish to consider sourcing from other suppliers that may value the government's business more highly. Potential exists here for governments to establish local supplier communities. Suppliers may assess the value of the government's business in terms of the volume and profit margin associated with the account, the potential for growth, opportunities to develop capabilities and efficiencies in systems, transaction processing (including electronic commerce), technology and inventory management, the level of communication that the buyer is willing to engage in about needs and performance feedback, as well as the profile of the client.

...reduce transaction costs and risks;

The supplier may regard the government as an account with development potential. The supplier may see possible opportunities for more valuable business in the future or consider the account to be high profile. In any case, the supplier may be willing, in the short-term at least, to meet the government's requirements in order to win more business. There can be many supplier development opportunities in these cases by seeking to improve the capacity and performance of these suppliers. Where the government is seen as a beneficial account, the supplier may have a high volume of sales; but the account is still regarded as unattractive perhaps due to low profitability, location, or inconvenience. Suppliers may be eager to increase prices. The government may wish to seek alternative suppliers or try to make the relationship more attractive by considering more efficient ways of transacting business. If the government's account is seen as a core part of the supplier's business, in most cases, a rewarding business relationship that seeks to continually add value can be established. The supplier is generally anxious to meet the buyer's requests and provide a high level of service in order to retain the account.

Understanding Departmental Procurement Capacities

*T*o effectively determine the capacity of procurement to deliver the needed goods and services, there must be clearly defined roles and responsibilities among the various service delivery units. Typically, this includes examining the activities procurement currently manages and identifying the administrative arrangements of the procurement function.

In order to adequately assess current strategies, benchmarks must be determined. NIGP has prepared a report of procurement practices based upon an extensive survey of member agencies. The database provides an opportunity for comparison with other public entities. Some of the common benchmarks used by procurement organizations include:

- number of certified professionals in the organization (may be expressed as a percentage of professional staff);
- number of cooperative/piggy-back bids;
- number of faxed bids/proposals;
- number of electronic bids/proposals;
- number of non-contract purchase orders issued for a given time frame;
- a purchasing process time report;
- number of long-term contracts issued for a given time period;
- number of purchase orders placed against long-term contracts for a given time period;
- average dollars per purchase order;
- frequency and quantity per purchase order for a given commodity;
- number of rush orders required;
- number of emergency orders;
- number of change orders;
- number of purchase orders per buyer;

- cost of a purchase order;
- number of term contracts allowed to expire;
- number of vendors;
- cost reductions achieved;
- cost of purchasing as a percentage of overall budget; and
- amount of budget expended with targeted suppliers (minority and women-based enterprises, recycled, local, etc.).

Although this is not a complete list of potential comparison targets, it provides a starting point for evaluating the department's purchasing activities and capabilities.

Projecting Procurement Expenditures

*I*f a procurement profile is available, trends in particular spend categories can be extrapolated, where some expenditures in the near future may become self-evident while others are decreasing. Graphing expenditure categories and continuing on with the trend line provides a quick and, in most cases, reliable indicator of short-term spend (1-3 years). Forecasting spending patterns can take the form of simple judgmental forecasts to more sophisticated econometric forecasts. Judgmental techniques, such as visual trend analysis and incremental modeling, provide a useful and relatively simple method for estimating short-term spend patterns. Other general and relatively easy techniques are the use of a moving average, exponential smoothing, and time-series regression. These techniques provide more robust accounting for changes but may be no more accurate in the short term than more simple judgmental techniques when variations in spend have not been significant.

Projecting long-term (longer than 3 years) spend patterns is much more difficult. A primary source of information can be obtained from key individuals within departments/agencies who can accurately project the department's/agency's expenditure and demand for goods and services. Decreasing or increasing expenditure patterns identified by key personnel indicating the nature of purchased goods or services may influence the future level of procurement effort and procurement strategies applied.

Providing information on anticipated significant purchases can also be used as part of a supplier development strategy. Local suppliers may be able to use this information to manage production and delivery schedules and determine new product lines and marketing strategies, making them better able to compete in the marketplace. It may also encourage new suppliers to enter the market. The information can also assist current suppliers in adjusting their production scheduling and delivery processes, which may reduce prices.

Establishing Performance Measurement and Monitoring Systems

*I*t goes without saying that performance measurement is crucial to any core public sector activity, program, department, or organization. If an activity is not measured against some established performance criteria (metric), then the management of resources can not be evaluated based upon some pre-defined criteria, and sustainable strategic improvements cannot be made. This is valid for both the entire organization as well as procurement. In fact, Fung (1999) found that the best procurement departments are able to measure and demonstrate their performance in areas, such as the efficiency of their own internal operations, the savings and contributions makes to the overall organization, including the measurement of customer satisfaction and the ability to benchmark process or outcomes, both internally, such as benchmarking against other departments, and externally, against some private or non-profit sector organizations.

There is a range of methods an organization can use to measure procurement performance. Some of the most common methods include performance reviews, regular staff meetings, benchmarking, performance indicators, performance targets, and quality management tools. Also, the concept of out-sourcing the procurement function is beginning to receive some attention. Perhaps the most common way in which procurement performance is conducted is through some general performance review process, typically during the budget cycle. There needs to be a dedicated, cross-cutting review of the procurement function to examine how procurement is conducted for all service delivery agencies of an organization. Ultimately, procurement should be judged as a tool for achieving service delivery outcomes.

It is generally believed that those best able to evaluate whether service delivery performance measure outcomes are being achieved, and to what level of achievement, are individual staff members who help deliver the products or services. If these products or services are not delivered to the customer's satisfaction, questions may be raised regarding potential procurement processes that may have contributed to the way in which customers viewed the delivery of individual products or services. Some of the common performance indicators are highlighted on Figure 16.

I. Cost Reduction and Containment (especially where demand is increasing, such as technology):

    • level of savings due to new contract/supplier arrangements or purchasing initiatives;

    • value of negotiated additional benefits;

    • cost reduction due to using alternative goods or services;

    • value of improved warranties;

    • reduced stock holdings and improved payment terms;

    • savings due to improved waste management; and

    • reduction in demand for a good or service.

II. Supplier and Industry Development:

    • targets to identify potential local suppliers;

    • numbers of firms involved in local supplier development programs; and

    • numbers of new sources of particular goods and services.

III. Supplier Performance

    • include a range of cost targets; and

    • gauge whether contract requirements, service, and quality requirements are met.

IV. Efficiency of Internal Procurement Systems and Processes Volume of Procurement Spend Transacted Electronically, or Through Other Transaction Methods Like P-cards:

    • volume of transactions transacted through aggregated or standing-offer arrangements;

    • reduction in transaction and inventory management costs and distribution costs;

    • internal customer satisfaction with devolution of purchasing processes and service levels;

    • response time and perceived value for money; and

    • perceived degree of simplicity, convenience, and effectiveness of procurement decision making and authority lines, systems, and processes.

Figure 16 - *Performance indicators by source.*

Source: Adapted from the *Corporate Procurement Planning*, Queensland State Government, Department of Public Works, Queensland Purchasing Division (February, 2001).

In some cases, it may be possible to gauge the direct contribution towards the achievement of organizational goals and objectives, e.g., growth in the number of local firms and the development of existing firms (increased activity/turnover and staffing levels) that may be attributable to the procurement function.

Another way to look at performance measurement and management is to use the supply-positioning table to establish target objectives for each quadrant. Quadrant I would be classified as low relative costs and low relative risk of securing supplies; and, therefore, some of the objectives may be a reduction in transaction costs by a given percentile, while Quadrant II would be relative low costs, but higher supply risk, where an objective might be increasing suppliers by developing a small business development program. Quadrant III would be high costs and low risks, where an objective may be cost pooling. Quadrant IV would be high cost and high risks, where the objective could be reduction of costs by 5%. For each quadrant, specific objectives can be established that can effectuate the development of performance measures.

Conclusion

A formal, well-written strategic procurement plan brings together a range of information collected throughout the process and makes it readily available to everyone in the organization. Generally, it is more than a collection of goal, objective, and strategy statements. The plan operates as an important management tool, since it lays out a panoramic, long-term agency-wide view. It conveys the procurement agency's priorities for a given planning horizon—typically, five years. It presents an easily understood, concise statement of strategic direction that contains enough detail to guide both long-term decision-making and short-term day-to-day procurement operations.

A formal plan also provides every employee involved in the process an understanding of the agency's direction, the rationale behind it, and an outline of how the agency will get there. It tells what is fundamentally important. Based on this understanding, organizational units determine how their work supports the plan. Smaller segments of the agency have the responsibility of translating the broad, aggregate agency view into daily operations. An agency's ability to reach its goals depends on its ability to build this linkage. The worth of a plan is tied to its role in agency management, guiding discussions, and influencing decisions within the entire agency.

When a procurement agency produces its plan, it may uncover certain issues that it must address to appropriately link the strategic procurement plan to actual agency operations. When it discusses these issues and clearly decides how the relationships will operate, it increases the likelihood that those who develop and implement the yearly action plan will succeed. An action plan describes what must occur, who must do it, and when it must be completed. It translates strategic actions into a yearly implementation plan. When the agency finishes a strategic plan, its thoughts should immediately turn to implementation. An agency has some important tools it can use to execute its plan. One of the most powerful is budget development. Its budgeting process should follow its strategic thinking and act as a tool to support strategic actions. An agency budget should reflect its strategic direction. Budgets crafted in the absence of strategic thought may not support the mission, mandates, and/or needs of key constituents effectively; and critical issues may not be addressed or managed sensibly.

References

Frayer, D. J., & Monczka, R. M. (1997). Enhanced strategic competitiveness through global supply chain management. *Annual Conference of the Council of Logistics Management,* 433-441.

Freeman, V., & Cavinato, J. (1990). Fitting purchasing to the strategic firm: Frameworks, processes, and values. *Journal of Purchasing and Materials Management, 26*(1), 19-25.

Fung, P. (1999). Managing purchasing in a supply chain context—Evolution and revolution. *Logistics Information Management, 12,* 362-366.

MacManus, S. (1992). *Doing business with government: Federal, state, local and foreign government purchasing practices for every business and public institution.* New York: Paragon House.

McHugh, M. (1997). Trouble in paradise: Disintegrated strategic change within a government agency. *International Journal of Public Sector Management, 10* (6), 433-443.

National Institute of Governmental Purchasing (NIGP) (2000). *Public procurement management.* Herndon, VA: National Institute of Governmental Purchasing.

Quayle, M. (1998). The impact of strategic procurement in the UK government sector. *International Journal of Public Sector Management, 11,* 397-413.

Rink, D. R., & Fox, H. W. (1999). Strategic procurement planning across the product's sales cycle: A conceptualization. *Journal of Marketing Theory and Practice, 7,* 28-42.

CHAPTER 4

Linking Resource Allocation Decisions to the SP² Process

*T*o most people budgeting is a mysterious process—even to a number of procurement professionals working in government. Most people are aware that the chief executive is responsible for proposing a budget to the legislative body and that the legislative body, in turn, makes decisions on taxes and what programs will receive financial support. If they work in government, they know that various supporting documents are prepared to justify "the budget" and that detailed controls exist which often inhibit simple management discretion. In the personal lives of most people, the family budget is a source of tension because of the need to live within one's income. Most people assume that public budgeting must deal with similar circumstances but that it must involve much more complex accounting and financial management techniques.

The purpose of this chapter is to inform procurement professionals about public sector budgeting. Much of the mystery associated with budgeting can be dispelled through careful identification of the budget process and clarification of the language of budgeting. Like any other activity that generates its own "language," budgeting is really a political process for determining who pays for government goods and services and who receives the goods and services that government provides.

One of the mysteries stems from a lack of conceptual clarity in defining public budgeting. A term can be defined by seeking out the common usages, or one can create a definition of one's own intellectual and conceptual purposes. The former approach is particularly useful when one is trying to understand the various perspectives that people bring to a given activity. The latter approach is useful when one is attempting to establish a reasonably uniform body of thought. Both approaches are employed herein.

Budgetary Perspectives

*T*here are many perspectives from where one can view public budgeting, and no one perspective is exclusively "correct." The most important perspectives are those of the politician, the economist, the accountant, the public manager, and the citizen. Given a democratic society, the budget is a tool used to frame the public policy debate; thus, the politician's perspective is important. Both economists and accountants have professional perspectives that greatly influence how we understand budgeting and how we believe we should practice budgeting. Economists provide theories and techniques which help define how budgeting should be accomplished (normative theories), what factors should be examined when allocating resources, and how to weigh these factors in making budget policy decisions. Accountants provide conceptual frameworks in which to execute and evaluate budgets, while citizens provide the support for or non-support for tax and allocation decisions. Ultimately, public procurement professionals must understand each of these perspectives when managing the affairs of government through the strategic procurement process.

The budgetary process can be viewed as a political event conducted in the political arena for political advantage. As any one in the trenches will attest, politics—being a reflection of human nature—has its best and worst sides. In some instances, politicians or individuals who influence politicians (such as the supplier community) are seeking money for themselves. In other instances, the political advantage sought is to further some ethical position or altruistic motives of key politicians. Motivations differ, but seeking political advantage through the budgetary process is constant. Thus, one significant perspective on budgeting is political.

Economists view budgetary decisions with the assumption that budget decisions are made within limited financial conditions and that rational analysis can, therefore, help identify the best decisions. Every budget decision involves potential benefits, which may or may not be obtained. It also involves "opportunity cost." If the available money is spent for one program, then another program is not funded or is funded at a lower level. In other words, opportunities are lost in every budget decision and there never seems to be enough money for every program. When choices have to be made, economic analysis can help one to evaluate the comparative benefits and costs, including opportunity cost. This view of budgeting focuses upon decision making and places a high premium upon the value of analysis in helping decision makers make "better" decisions.

Accountants stress the importance of capturing accurate financial information. To the accountant, the budget is the statement of desired policy, and information on actual expenditures is compared to the budget to judge whether policy has been followed, as well as to question the wisdom of the original policy. The accountant's view largely defines how public managers understand how they should execute the budget and how some of their evaluators will judge their actions.

Citizens often view the budget as a battle between competing forces, usually along party lines. In many cases, the only time citizens become active participants in budget deliberations is if tax increases are proposed or programs are to be cut. They tend to view the budget as an obfuscated process where bureaucrats vie for position and politicians receive "pork." As a substantive policy document, citizens dismiss the budget process and, instead, often lobby specific legislators or agency directors for specific demands—leading to what Lowi (1969) identified as the Iron-Triangle.

None of these views—the politician, the economist, the accountant, or the citizen—is incorrect. Each perspective is valuable in getting a more comprehensive understanding of public budgeting. It is interesting that the perspective of the public procurement manager most closely approximates the storyteller in the parable of the three blind men. Public managers must try to achieve a more comprehensive view, but they cannot fall into the trap of arrogantly believing that such a view is anything more than one valid perspective among others.

Procurement has a strategic role to play in the budgeting process of the organization. At the operational level, this revolves around the development of the procurement budget. Complexity increases with participation in cost development for services by other departments and with the development of estimates for capital budgets. Effective budgeting means that enough resources will be available to meet the demands of the agency's constituents. In this way, budgeting entails aspects of planning and fiduciary relationships to ensure that sufficient cash resources will be available for allocation decisions when expenditure commitments are made.

It also includes the notion of cash management. When must operating expenses be paid during a given year? What is the expected amount of payments, which will need to be made to support operating or capital programs?

There are a host of financial questions like these that have critical implications for the governmental agency and procurement. If expenditures occur at a faster pace than the inflow of revenues to cover them, the agency must borrow. Since there are interest cost implications to borrowing, it is more costly to borrow in order to meet shortfalls than if cash flows are synchronized with expenditures. This relates to the cost of interest on borrowing, controlling costs, and overall financial management accountability.

The Budget Cycle in Government

...the budget cycle consists of four distinct phases: planning, formalization, implementation and evaluation.

Although there are many exceptions, public agencies in the U.S. usually commence their fiscal or budget year on October 1; other common fiscal years begin on January 1 or July 1. Even though they may have different fiscal years, all governments follow a common budget cycle. Consistent with the procurement cycle identified in Chapter 1, the budget cycle consists of four distinct phases: planning, formalization, implementation and evaluation.

Planning. This phase involves the estimation of the budget resources and anticipated expenditures. During the preparation phase, the chief executive estimates the revenues and expenditures for the budget period. The individual department units are the sources of many of these estimates. It is also in this phase that procurement may be called upon to provide estimates of the costs of various items and services needed by the governmental unit. At the end of the planning phase, a proposed budget document is prepared for submission to the governing body.

At the start of the budget cycle, budget instructions are prepared for distribution to the various participants to help with the development of the budget. The *Budget Message* is a communication normally written by the chief executive that accompanies the budget estimate. The purpose of the transmittal letter or budget message is to explain:

- the main points of the budget;
- the assumptions under which it was assembled; and
- the major policy recommendations.

The budget instructions include the fiscal and policy guidelines and submission worksheets that the departments must complete. Typically, departments must return a narrative description of their department or program objectives, service delivery plans, staffing levels, cost/benefit analyses, and specific dollar requests. At the end of the preparation phase, a budget document for the agency is prepared, which includes summaries of estimated receipts and outflows of all funds, the actual cash position of the agency, and any borrowing and repayment schedules. This is often supplemented with a formal budget review process at the midyear point. Both budget preparation and the subsequent midyear review form part of the overall strategic planning process.

Because of the amount of time and resources spent preparing and adopting budgets, some agencies are using biennial or two-year budgets to save preparation time in future years. In the non-budget year, preparation time can be spent on more detailed analysis of specific departments or programs.

Formalization. Adoption is the approval of the budget by the governing body of the entity. This phase involves the legal adoption of the expenditure and revenue projections. It may involve various public hearings where the details of the budget are discussed, and occasionally the legislating body needs to pass interim budgets in order to ensure that government operations continue while budgets are being deliberated. To rectify this problem, some governments have passed statutory provision for the automatic, temporary continuation of funding (based on the previous year's levels of spending) in the event that budget approvals are delayed.

In preparation for adoption, the chief executive prepares an executive budget summary or set of budget estimates that were developed in the planning phase for submission to the governing body. After extensive discussion, the governing body approves the Acts, Appropriation Orders or Ordinances, which constitute the legal basis for the ensuing budget period expenditures. This includes the division of the budget into broad spending categories, often called budget allotments, votes, or envelopes.

The adoption process authorizes revenues and expenditures for the fiscal period. Most appropriations lapse at the end of the fiscal period. Without tight discipline and strict control, this can lead to a "spend it or lose it" syndrome (Petersen & Strachota, 1991, p. 54). It is ironic that efforts to maximize financial control through lapsing appropriations can actually provide an incentive for inefficient use of resources. To counteract this tendency, some agencies have developed various savings programs that allow departments to use 50% or even 100% of unspent appropriations by a re-appropriation process for the next fiscal period. Many capital budgets allow those funds to be carried over multiple fiscal years until the specific capital project is completed. In other cases, agencies have enforced strict controls over spending on specific items in order to curb year-end spending sprees, e.g., no spending on desktop computers and related items after the third quarter of the fiscal year.

In order to closely link program expectations to results and to "let managers manage," some governing bodies are beginning to make lump sum appropriations where dollars are authorized for a stated purpose, budget unit, or category of expenditure without detailed specification for their use. The chief executive or department managers are given the necessary resources, authority, and responsibility to spend prudently. The reason for making appropriations is to provide resources to pursue program goals. Providing lump sum flexibility in the use of monies allows decision makers to maximize program effectiveness. Operational managers can adapt inputs to meet needs by relinquishing stringent financial control, for example, of a line item expenditure appropriation.

Implementation. Implementation is the execution of the budget during the budget period. It involves collecting revenues and expending the proceeds for the purposes intended. Implementation involves allotting and allocating when expenditures can be made. Allotments control the rate of spending authorized by an appropriation. An allocation controls specific use of the monies appropriated. The chief executive can divide an appropriation into time frames when it will be spent during the fiscal year. Each allotment determines the limit of a budget unit's legal authority (viz. the amount of funding available) to incur obligations and make expenditures within the stated time frame. Care should be taken to match allotments to demand for services and not just spread them equally to all budget units, e.g., matching seasonal demand for services with the ability to pay for those services that can be determined in the cash management forecast.

Evaluation. This part of the budget cycle involves reviewing the budget. Periodic reports should be prepared showing how much of the budget has been spent to date. Other monitoring methods include pre-authorization requisitions by the budget office or procurement to ensure adequate funds to pay for the purchase. In addition, the use of accrual accounting systems is becoming more manifest. Evaluation assesses the results of the budget. This phase of the budget cycle includes monitoring various budget reports and conducting and publishing performance audit results. This may include financial and compliance audits as well as economy and efficiency audits. (Audit types will be discussed later in this chapter.)

One reason that many are confused about public budgeting is that during any given fiscal year (remember that fiscal years are not necessarily consistent with calendar years), all four phases of the budget process are occurring. For instance, if the fiscal year is 2010-2011, during this year the planning for year 2012-2013 would be conducted; the formalization of 2011-2012 would be passed; the 2010-2011 budget would be implemented; and the 2009-2010 budget would be evaluated. The next fiscal year (2011-2012) would follow the same logic. The 2010-2011 budget would be evaluated; the 2012-2013 budget would be formalized; the 2013-2014 budget would be in the initial stages of planning; and the 2011-2012 budget would be implemented.

What is a Good Budget?

No two budget documents are exactly the same. They vary by laws and traditions, which affect both the budgetary process, as well and as the resultant document. Budgeting has also been said to be more like art than science; therefore, each budget is unique to the artist. The Government Finance Officers Association (GFOA) currently has a Budget Award program that identifies the specific standards that are to be used in evaluating budgets. The process used by GFOA evaluates a budget in four ways: as a policy *document,* as an *operations guide,* as a *financial plan,* and as a *communication device.*

As a policy document, a budget should articulate the program priorities and goals. This would include stating economic and policy assumptions on which the budget is based. The operations guide component shows the allocation of resources and the performance objectives and measures of the various departments, programs, or activities. The financial plan goes into the sources of revenue and any debt financing. As communication devices, budgets should act as a stimulus for conversations and dialogue by the public on the important budget issues. Budgets-in-brief are increasingly popular forms of budget, which give citizens a guide to the budget, but in a summary or highly condensed version. However, they also clearly state how to get more detailed information. Some jurisdictions have also begun to make budget videos and use other electronic means to get the word out on the budget.

Budgetary Funds

Good budgets also include the proper division of the budget(s) into the common accounting structure. This is accomplished by separating various budgets by fund types. Generally Accepted Accounting Principles promulgated by the General Accounting Standards Board call for seven types of funds which can be grouped into three broad categories: governmental funds; proprietary funds; and fiduciary funds.

A fund is an independent legal fiscal entity with assets; liabilities; reserves; a residual balance, or equity; and revenues and expenditures for undertaking activities. Funds may be expendable, meaning the authorization for spending expires at the end of the fiscal period; or non-expendable or revolving, meaning that spending beyond the fiscal year is allowed without reauthorization. Generally Accepted Accounting Principles establish the uniform criteria (accounting standards) for how state and local governments are to account and record their financial operations, which include all the necessary regulations, rules, policies, and procedures that define accepted accounting principles.

Governmental funds generally finance the activities most citizens associate with general-purpose governments, e.g., police, fire, education, public works, and procurement. These funds also support activities, which cannot easily be assigned to other funds. Proprietary funds are used to account for activities that are intended to be operated and financed similar to private businesses, e.g., water and wastewater funds, other utility funds, and/or some recreation funds. Fiduciary funds, such as pension funds, are intended to account for assets held by a governmental unit in a trustee capacity. Governmental funds may be further subdivided into four categories.

- The **general fund** is used to track revenues and expenditures that support all services not assigned to other funds. This may include police, fire, finance, procurement, and other administrative support functions.
- **Special revenue funds** provide services financed from various specifically designated revenue sources, such as recreation fees used to support a specific recreation activity.
- **Capital project funds** are used to acquire major assets with a useful life of more than one year, which may be financed by some form of long-term debt.

- **Debt service funds** receive resources from other funds, taxes, grants or proceeds from long-term debt and are used to pay the principal and interest on the debt.

Proprietary funds include two types of funds—enterprise and internal service funds that are used when governments engage in activities similar to private businesses.

- **Internal service funds** are used by governmental organizations that provide services to other units within the government by charging fees for services rendered to cover costs of operating the service. Examples of this include data services, warehousing, procurement, and administrative service fees. These funds should provide services to consumers and/or other governmental units at a price that covers both the current cost of operation and the financing necessary for capital assets.

- **Enterprise funds** control various types of utilities (water, water reclamation, storm water, electric) and other entities providing service financed through user charges.

Fiduciary funds are those where the government acts as a custodian of assets that must be disbursed to individual, private and public entities, and other funds. Examples include pension funds and collecting lottery proceeds for distribution to others.

Types of Budgets

Once the various types of funds have been determined, they can then be used in the two common budget types: operating and capital budgets. Operating budgets include all the revenues and expenditures to cover the current fiscal period of the government. The annual operating budget provides the vehicle through which the governing body establishes the authorization of the government to spend money during a specific time period for specific purposes and the economic resources that will be required to support those expenditures. Capital budgets cover the outlays for major acquisitions of long-term assets, such as infrastructure construction of buildings, roads, and utility systems. Most capital expenditures have two aspects in common: a long useful life and are infrequent and expensive.

A term that is sometimes used interchangeably with capital budget is Capital Improvement Program (CIP); however, a CIP program is a multiyear plan that forecasts spending for all anticipated capital projects. The capital budget is the legal document which authorizes spending for specific projects during the ensuing fiscal period. Effective CIPs include the location, scale, and timing of needed capital projects and how the projects are to be financed. A typical capital improvement planning process would include the following steps:

- identify proposed projects;
- consider all proposed projects simultaneously;
- produce a planning document that considers both financing sources and the timing of when the projects should be built;
- involve some ranking process based on perceived community need, net present value, and/or internal rate of return of the investment in the project;
- analyze source of funding for projects which may include:
  - pay-as-you-go from current income;
  - grants;
  - debt financing; and
  - public/private ventures, including privatization.

Procurement has several key roles in any capital improvement process and the capital budget. First, procurement should be involved in the process to estimate the various costs to provide a capital project. Procurement has a unique perspective, not only on what it takes to construct a project, but also on ongoing costs for care and maintenance. Procurement can help with estimates of Operating and Maintenance costs (O&M) for each capital project. The role of procurement also extends to the development of life-cycle costing of the project from its inception and encouraging selected contractors to use value analysis techniques. Finally, part of contract management entails ensuring the agency adheres to its budget and project plan.

Capital budgeting also includes major purchases of equipment. The threshold and rules for determining what is O&M and what is capital vary from agency to agency. For example, in a small city, police patrol cars may be in the capital budget; while, in a large city, they may be part of the normal operating expenses and considered recurring expenditures. Procurement should constantly review the list of major capital equipment purchases. Besides providing detailed estimates after the budget is approved, Procurement should group similar purchases together for economic buys, including searching for possibilities for cooperative buys and advising on the timing of the purchases for most economic buys. Procurement must also ensure the equipment is delivered when needed. Delivery timing considerations include such concerns as vehicle production cutoff dates.

Budget Approaches

*B*udget systems provide a means to evaluate competing demands for resources and a system to measure objectives to be obtained in meeting the goals of the organization. There are three purposes of public budgeting, which are often seen as being in dynamic tension with one another: goal attainment, financial control, and managerial accountability. The different approaches—rational, line item, performance, program, zero-based budgets, and results-oriented budgeting—reflect variations in the political context or realities of these three purposes.

Rational Budget Decision Model. Drawing heavily upon the economists' views of budgets, if budgeting is the allocation of scarce resources among competing demands, how can decisions be made that will generate the greatest net benefits for the dollars expended? It has been stated that the rational budget model is the most effective budgetary approach for realizing goals that mirror public preferences and values. Since the economic theory of budgeting is designed to tie dollars expended directly to outcomes or benefits, the rational models in budget decision making can promote economic efficiency by allocating resources to those programs and services that both generate greater net benefits and result in incremental benefits greater than the incremental costs.

According to Aronson (1996), the rational budget decision model to judge efficiency in budget dollar allocations uses a set of three criteria: intersector, interprogram, and intraprogram efficiency. **Intersector efficiency** questions whether or not the cost of government activity yields more benefits to society than if it remained in the private sector. A typical example is daycare. Should it be provided by the agency as a government service, or should it be left to the private sector? **Interprogram efficiency** judges competing programs and allocates the resources to the program that produce the greatest net benefits. Should the police budget for youth activities be increased, or should youth programs in recreation be increased? **Intraprogram efficiency** within each program should combine the resources to maximize the net benefits from any given expenditure increment. For example, would it be more efficient for a specific service to be performed in-house or contracted out?

The rational decision model is quite comprehensive and complex from a public policy perspective. It involves several steps:

- Evaluate the social needs in order to develop objective programs to meet them.

- Assign each objective a monetary value representing the benefit to be gained by achieving it.

- Develop criteria to select the best alternative, and choose which program to finance.

- Determine which program to finance based on available resources. Select options above and below current funding.

- Calculate the costs to be incurred, both socially and financially, and the benefits.

- Compare programs and select the ones for funding that yield the greatest additional benefits for the additional costs.

In contrast to its strengths, the major weaknesses of a rational budget approach are that:

- It maybe difficult to quantify the costs and benefits of programs.

- It is difficult to reach consensus among decision makers.

- There are significant administrative time and cost burdens for analysis and implementation.

Line-Item Budgeting. Line-item budgeting is the oldest and still the predominant form of budgeting in the public sector. Line-item budgets are considerably easier to prepare and implement than other budget types, such as performance, program, or zero-based budgets. They are also more easily understood by decision makers, providing guidance on what and how managers are to spend. Line-item budgets tend to stress the accountants' perspectives, although politicians often prefer this form because of the line-item veto power it provides.

Line-item budgets focus directly on the commodities and services to be bought. Appropriations are approved for different classes of expenditure, such as personal services and supplies (see Figure 17). Budgets can be further divided into subclasses, such as salary, overtime, and even separate items such as compensation for individual positions. Funding for purchases can be easily broken down into specific groups of commodities and services. This form of budgeting was developed in response to the widespread governmental corruption that prevailed at the turn of the Twentieth Century. It was designed specifically to maximize control and to ensure financial accountability.

Personnel Services
- Salaries – Permanent
- Salaries – Hourly
- Salaries – Overtime
- Employee Benefits
    - Life Insurance
    - Health Insurance
    - Retirement
    - Disability Insurance
    - Workers Compensation Insurance
    - Unemployment Insurance

Contractual Services
- Telephone
    - Internet
    - Voice Mail
    - Long distance charges
- Postage
- Advertising
- Utility Charges
    - Electric
    - Natural Gas
    - Water
    - Waste Water
- Reproduction Expenses
    - Copy Machines
    - Printing
- Internal Service Charges
    - Computer Service Department fees
- Training
    - Seminar fees
    - Subscriptions
    - Professional dues

Commodities
- Office Supplies

Capital
- Computers
- Furniture
- Office Equipment

Figure 17 - *Typical line items.*

Line items are fixed budgets with monies appropriated only for a particular time period, usually one year. The major weaknesses of line-item budgets are:

- This type of budget focuses on what is purchased rather than the achievement of goals.

- There are no criteria for evaluating funding because the chief executive does not know what is to be gained or lost by increasing or decreasing expenditures.

- Efficient trade-offs among services are impossible to determine and must be made on the basis of subjective judgments on service effectiveness.

- Line-item budgets are prone to incremental increase in successive fiscal periods without regard for whether additional resources will result in improved service delivery.

- Line-item budgets also encourage spend-it-or-lose-it attitudes, which may result in an end of fiscal year rush to spend remaining budget allocations.

Performance Budgeting. Performance budgets relate expenditures and revenues to workloads (miles of streets to sweep or tons of refuse to collect). They were developed in the 1940s after a Hoover Commission report on U.S. federal government budgeting. This type of budget was viewed as a mechanism to improve the management of service delivery, with cost efficiency being the principal indicator of managerial effectiveness. In the performance budget approach, government activities are divided into major functions, each encompassing those programs that further the goals of the agency. In turn, programs are made up of a number of activities that are undertaken by separate performance units. A unit may be an entire department or a division work group. Any one unit may be responsible for more than one activity (Figure 18).

Mission

Our mission is to serve the citizens of Clearwater by effective coordination of the fiscal management of the City through effectively providing timely, responsive, and comprehensive financial/support services to all our customers.

Description of Services

The department is organized into the following programs. The Finance program performs administration, accounting, treasury, payroll and purchasing functions. The Risk Management program administers the City's self-insurance program which includes general liability, commercial property, and Workers' Compensation.

Strategic Objectives/Measures/and Targets

Strategic Priority	Objective	Measure
Infrastructure Maintenance and Improvements	Maintain/improve the City's General Obligation Bond (GOB) and other bond ratings	Bond ratings

Performance 2001/02: S&P Moody's Fitch

	S&P	Moody's	Fitch
01 Imp Rev Ref	A	A2	
02 Water/Sewer		A2	A
02 Stormwater	A	A3	A
02 Sports Complex	A	A2	

Strategic Priority	Objective	Measure
Economic Development/ Public Saftely	Increase use of Purchasing Cards to insure continued ability to efficiently provide resources for city operations	Actual rebate amount received from use of purchasing cards

Performance 2001/02:
$6,293.95

# of purchasers using cards
Performance 2001/02
Active accounts 436

Strategic Priority	Objective	Measure
Infrastructure Maintenance and Improvements	Minimize the cost of issuing debt	Yield of bonds compared to market yield

Performance 2001/02:

01 Improvement Rev Ref	3.17%	(5 yr)
Market	3.35%	(5 yr)
02 Water/Sewer Rev Ref	3.04%	(5 yr)
Market	3.20%	(5 yr)
02 Stormwater Rev Ref	2.64%	(5 yr)
Market	2.91%	(5 yr)
01 Sports Complex	2.63%	(5 yr)
Market	2.91%	(5 yr)

Figure 18 - *Performance budget—Example.*

City of Clearwater, Florida
(http://www.myclearwater.com/gov/depts/finance/mission.asp)

Outputs or end-product measures are developed for each activity of a performance unit. The performance unit manager considers different mixes of objects of expenditure entailing different costs and different levels of output. The goal is to select the alternative that yields the lowest unit cost. The manager estimates the number of units multiplied by the unit cost figures to arrive at the requested budget amount. Along with the budget amount requested, the manager prepares a narrative statement that:

- describes how each activity pertains to the unit's service responsibilities and goals;
- outlines the tasks to be performed in carrying out each activity;
- demonstrates how the appropriations will facilitate each activity; and
- sets forth a work plan that specifies milestones for output units to be accomplished and type and amount of work to reach milestones.

Collecting data on the outputs and determining if milestones are met are approaches for monitoring this type of budget. Major weaknesses of performance budgets include the following:

- Unit cost measures are not always meaningful indicators of progress toward goals.
- Separated activities assigned to performance units may not include all the organizational actions that contribute to a particular output.
- If the program format is superimposed on the existing organizational structure, the cost centers may not correspond to responsibility centers.

Thus, total costs may not be compiled accurately, and unit cost can become a misleading indicator of cost efficiency. For example, a municipality's efforts on behalf of at-risk youth might be broken out in recreation programs in the Parks and Recreation budget as well as by special programs for at-risk youth in the police department.

- Benefits are not measured, as there are no indicators of intersector efficiency.
- Interprogram efficiency cannot be established, because unit cost does not indicate the net value yielded by each program.

Funding requests for each activity consist of only a single estimate based on lowest unit cost. Performance budgeting does not facilitate interprogram efficiency. The chief executive cannot make decisions on the basis of net benefits that would be gained or lost by shifting resources.

Program Budgeting. Program budgets relate expenditures and revenues to public goals. The Planning, Programming, and Budgeting Systems (PPBS) are the most elaborate form of program budgeting. It was developed by the U.S. federal government for use in the 1960s, and a scaled-down version was adopted for use by some local governments.

Chief executives designate organizational goals at the beginning of the program budget process. Goals have a program structure designed to prescribe how those goals will be achieved. During the budget process, past budgetary commitments are re-examined to determine whether resources should be reallocated to new programs. The adopted program budget is designed to have the greatest net benefit for the cost. This type of budget tends to be more long range with multiyear plans prepared along with budget requests. This allows a review of revenue and expenditures for many years in the future in order to identify potential resources and demands so that future funding needs can be determined. Managers of program budgets are accountable for comparing targets in the budget plan with actual achievement of objectives and program results. Managers can adjust programs when changes occur that affect targets or workload requirements.

Program Budget - Example

BUDGET BY PROGRAM	2000-2001 ACTUAL	2001-2002 BUDGET	2001-2002 ESTIMATE	2002-2003 BUDGET
TOTAL DEPARTMENT	$6,052,996	$6,024,409	$6,084,917	$6,607,914
Administration	756,285	810,305	806,860	743,839
Emergency Services	4,389,079	4,173,710	4,208,686	4,394,329
Resource Management (Support Services)	169,007	358,860	375,318	606,616
Fire Prevention	251,626	250,707	256,191	268,247
Medical Services	204,134	216,265	223,863	328,216
Community Relations	143,163	59,770	54,849	60,125
Training	66,202	68,322	66,218	70,296
Hazardous Materials	73,375	78,770	90,232	127,546
Civil Defense	125	8,700	2,400	8,700

Figure 19 - *Program budget—Example.*

As an example, one agency performed a study on its alternative transportation program. The goal of the program was to reduce vehicle travel miles by 10% over the base year. The study was to determine if the methods employed and the dollars expended for the program were indeed having an effect. A word of caution on such studies is that often a program may be effective, but it has not had sufficient time to mature and meet the required goals. Thus, there is a danger that a good program could be cut prematurely. The major weaknesses of program budgets are:

- Goals are difficult to define and formulate.
- Goals are subject to change, and the programs must change when goals change.
- For some goals, it is impossible to obtain objective measures of benefits and objectives.
- Systemic evaluation of alternatives is subject to human limitations and time and cost constraints.

Zero-Based Budgeting. Zero-Based Budgets (ZBB) relate expenditures and revenues to workloads and organize allocation decisions according to "decision packets" of cost centers for which alternative levels of service delivery can be specified. Decision packets are ranked by relative importance to allow the elimination of entire packages. ZBB reflects (through the use of alternative service levels and ranking procedures) an attempt to provide the chief executive and management with an alternative to incremental fiscal period funding increases. This form originated in the private sector and gained popularity with some governments in the 1970s. The Zero-Based Budget approach involves several steps:

- Establish decisions and units or subunits with a designated manager who has responsibility and authority over specific sets of activities. ZBB is not identified with a particular budget format. In a program format, the decision units would be the program elements (departments or divisions).
- Prepare decision packages, one for each alternative funding level. Each package identifies the mission and goals of the unit, the different ways to deliver services, and describes the benefits of each alternative. Funding levels go from the minimum, current and improved levels normally listed by percentages above and below current funding, i.e., 90%, 100%, 110%. The minimum level is the amount needed to keep the activities viable, usually in the 80-90% range.

- Rank the decision packages. The chief executive or another member of the management team selects packages to be funded starting with the highest ranked and continues until expenditure total equals the maximum allowable spending for the budget. This is then submitted to the governing body for adoption.

The major weaknesses of ZBB are:

- Most organizations will not give managers the required latitude needed to make ZBB work. Managers must be given flexibility to adapt to changes that affect cost and output levels.

- Without measurement of costs and benefits, the chief executive and governing body cannot judge the intersector or interprogram efficiency.

- Without a program structure, decision makers cannot conduct coherent analyses of alternatives. Since activities in several decision units may contribute to the same output, authority over services is diffused.

Results-Oriented Budgeting. In response to a growing demand by elected officials, citizens, and public managers to build accountability structures into the budget process, a new form of budgeting emerged in the twenty-first century. Results-oriented budgeting is budgeting that attempts to link resource allocations decisions to performance criteria that include both output and outcomes measures. Although there are many facets of performance based budgeting in the format, results-oriented budgeting adds a new wrinkle – performance measures that look at outcomes of activities rather than on simply outputs. Say, for example, you were looking at the sanitation department, one distinct measure may include tons of garbage collected (output) as well as a measure looking at citizens satisfaction with their garbage collection service (outcome).

Another distinction between performance based budgeting and results-oriented budgeting is that performance based budgeting focuses primarily on internally derived performance targets. Results-oriented budgeting must, in order to be effective, be linked to the overall strategic plan of the organization, and each decision unit (similar to the decision units in ZBB) must support a particular goal and objectives.

Budget Approach Summary

*T*he basic purpose of public budgeting is the efficient attainment of governmental goals. The rational budget model with its intersector, interprogram and intraprogram efficiency measures is the most effective for realizing goals that most closely reflect public preferences and values. The rational decision model incorporates elements of both program and zero-based budgeting. Line item budgets are the most popular and are easier to prepare and implement than the others. However, the other forms have advantages in shifting the focus of budgeting from financial control to strategic planning. The other forms do require large amounts of paperwork and administration time, high accounting information and analysis cost. For small, local governments this complexity and expense may be unnecessary. (Aronson, pp. 135-167)

Table 1

Comparison of Budget Approaches

(Ranked from 1 through 5 with 1
signifying the best approach and 5 being the worst)

	Implementation	Goal Attainment	Managerial Productivity	Financial Control
Rational	5	1	1	3
Line Item	1	4	4	1
Program	3	3	2	3
Performance	3	3	2	3
Zero-Based	3	5	4	3
Results-Oriented	4	5	5	2

In summary, the basic purpose of public budgeting is the efficient attainment of governmental goals. The rational budget model with its intersector, interprogram, and intraprogram efficiency measures is most effective for realizing goals that most closely reflect public preferences and values. The rational decision model incorporates elements of both program and zero-based budgeting. Line-item budgets are the most popular and are easier to prepare and implement than the others. However, the other forms have advantages in shifting the focus of budgeting from financial control to strategic planning. The other forms do require large amounts of paperwork and administration time, high accounting information, and analysis cost. For small, local governments, this complexity and expense may be unnecessary (Aronson, 1996, pp. 135-167).

Table 2

Comparison of Budget Approaches

(Ranked from 1 through 5 with 1
signifying the best approach and 5 being the worst)

	Implementation	Goal Attainment	Managerial Productivity	Financial Control
Rational	5	1	1	3
Line Item	1	4	4	1
Program	3	3	2	3
Performance	3	3	2	3
Zero-Based	3	5	4	3

In terms of these factors, it is obvious that no one approach to budgeting is perfect. For example, what may be the best approach in terms of goal attainment or managerial productivity is found wanting in terms of implementation or financial control. It appears that a blend of approaches will yield the best results.

Preparing an Operating Budget

*P*rocurement operations support other operations of the agency, and resources allocated to and within procurement must mirror the priorities of the jurisdiction. At the start of the budgeting process, the budget office of the agency prepares a policy overview. This includes a statement of the priorities and goals of the budget. It also details the economic and policy assumptions to be followed by departments in developing their budgets to include such things as new services the agency may be offering, any budget increases for these services or budget reductions for anticipated economic downturns, expected population increases or decreases, and interest rate factors to be utilized. All must be considered and included.

Regardless of the type of budget format used, estimates must be made to determine the resource requirements of the procurement department. It is simply the presentation format that will be different. Procurement must look at the services necessary to be provided to its direct customers in other departments, as well as to expectations from all other clientele. Estimates must then be made on the amount of staffing needed and the various items, services, and systems needed to support those procurement activities.

Determining Service Needs

What types of services are offered by the public agency as a whole? Each governmental agency has a unique blend of services and business plans to which procurement must respond. The spectrum of services may include education, health care, assisted living and full nursing care homes, care for the indigent and homeless, public safety, public utility services, streets, garbage collection, snow removal, beach preservation, library services, parks, and recreation.

The scope of the various programs of the agency and the services provided can be considered to be **Demand Measures.** These Demand Measures are an important component of preparing a budget. Some examples are: number of miles of street to pave, tons of refuse to collect, square miles of the service area, number of residences to serve by the fire department, and population to be served by police and other departments.

Workload Measures relate to the amount of work performed on a particular activity. Examples are often easier to arrive at for operational departments, such as number of fires or the number of garbage pickups, but procurement can also quantify number of bids, proposals, contracts administered, and surplus auctions, to name a few.

Procurement operations can determine service needs by evaluating the current requests that are being received from using agencies as well as historical experience. First, list what types of services are provided by procurement: requests for proposals, contract administration, surplus property, procurement card program, inventory and warehousing requirements. Some of the tools employed by procurement to meet the workload are blanket and term agreements, purchasing card programs, contract management, and request for proposal processes. A staffing plan can be developed based on the agency services and how procurement helps respond to these.

Estimating Staffing Needs

Full-time Equivalent Position (FTE). The baseline for estimating staffing requirements is a full-time position chart. The chart must adjust for part-time positions by converting them to an equivalent of a full-time position based on the standard of a 40-hour work week and on 2,080 hours of total work per year. For example, a part-time buyer working 20 hours per week would be the equivalent to .5 (20 * 52 weeks = 1,040 hours. 2080 hours/1040 hours = .5) of a full-time position.

To begin, first estimate the number of hours required to perform certain services. These estimates of hours can come from observation of workloads for a number of weeks and the amount of time required to perform certain tasks. Then, those hours can be extrapolated for an entire year. For example, if it takes a buyer an average of 40 hours to prepare bid specifications, manage the bid process, attend the pre-bid, open, and award a bid, by knowing the number of bids to be processed in a year and multiplying that number by 40 allows one to arrive at the number of hours necessary to perform that function. By dividing that number by 2080 (the average work hours in a full time equivalent), you would arrive at the number of FTEs required for that function. By calculating this formula for all functions, an ideal staffing compliment can be developed. The salary for each particular position along with the amount of employee benefits and other costs can then be calculated. Benefits are normally expressed as a percentage of the base salary; that standard percentage should be obtained from the human resources or financial departments of the agency.

it takes a buyer an average of 40 hours...

Most procurement agencies are not able to secure additional FTEs even if there is good justification for adding staff. When compared with services, such as fire, police, or direct human services delivery, support staff of all kinds are less valued than adding an additional firefighter or police officer. Some procurement agencies have begun to address their staffing needs by decentralizing functions, placing procurement personnel directly in using departments or even outsourcing. When the National Renewable Energy Laboratory (NREL) was faced with severe budget cuts, it developed plans to place procurement officers in the various departments that were supported by procurement. While the procurement officers' work continued to be supervised and performed in accordance with central procurement authority, the dollars to pay for the staff were included directly in the supported programs' budgets. A similar success was achieved by a municipality (City of Fort Collins, Colorado), which had been understaffed with increasing demands for procurement services. A senior buyer was placed with the utility department to provide additional requested procurement activities. The utility funded the senior buyer, freeing needed resources in the procurement division, which allowed an additional buyer to be hired. These and other creative means must be utilized by procurement in the future to ensure adequate personnel resources to perform effectively. Since most procurement operations are well below ideal staffing levels, there is a constant search for methods to add value to the procurement function while looking for improvements in efficiency (longer term agreements, raising of bid limits, etc.) to reduce and manage the workload.

Many agencies are beginning to develop an industrial funding approach to provide resources for procurement. The Federal Supply Service in the General Services Administration utilizes a percentage return on some scheduled purchase agreements. The funds received are used to pay for the operations that develop the supply contracts. Other examples include the rebates received on procurement card programs. These approaches make it more critical to provide quality, value-added services to ensure the viability of procurement operations in the future.

Estimating Operating Expenses

Typical line items which must be budgeted regardless of the budget format can generally be divided into the major categories of Personnel Services, Contractual Services, Commodities, and Capital Outlays. Procurement must determine what its operating budget needs are as well as provide information on the costs of various products and services which other departments need to complete their budgets. Most procurement departments have been in existence for many years and can rely on historical data to project future internal expenses. Training is one area that should not be overlooked in the procurement budget. Unfortunately, when budgets are under increasing pressure, one of the first items to be cut is training. It is often considered a frill; however, the ability to continue to do the job better is directly tied to learning and applying multiple skills. Reducing training budgets is shortsighted and, while it may not reduce the quality of services delivered next year, it will negatively impact performance in the future. Providing training and continuing professional development for procurement staff is an ongoing challenge for many managers.

Administering and Auditing the Budget

Once a budget is adopted, it must be actively monitored to ensure programs and activities are being accomplished within the budget resources allocated. One simple method of tracking available resources is to review budget expenditures on a monthly basis. Depending on the timing of expenditures throughout the year, a ballpark estimate of how the budget is being expended can be made. For example, if staffing levels are constant over the year, by reviewing salary expenditures, one would expect approximately 25% of salaries to be spent in the first quarter, with 75% remaining; 50% at six months, and 75% at three quarters, with 25% remaining. If these figures are out of balance, it may signal trouble in meeting the budget. The sooner this is known, the better, so that corrective action may be taken. This is true for all other expenditure categories, such as telephone and office supplies.

Additionally, expenditures must be monitored to ensure that all expenses are only incurred when planned, e.g., all telephone expenditures should not be made in the first quarter. If the training budget must last all year, it is important to identify which training will be needed and when. If all of a training budget is expended in the first quarter then other training needs are unmet.

Once the fiscal period has ended, active monitoring of the budget shifts to the audit and evaluation of the budget. Someone responsible for the financial affairs of the agency often oversees the audit function, although it may be reported directly to the head of an agency. Whether it is the comptroller or the budget manager, someone has the responsibility to manage financial risks, understand any financial implications of decisions, properly account for financial results, and guard against fraud, infractions on financial policies and principles, and loss of assets. Simply stated, someone in the organization must be the financial conscience. Audits are also performed to evaluate the budget. There are four types of audits:

- **Financial and compliance audits** are performed by an independent accounting firm with the main purpose of detecting of fraud. The Internal Audit group or Inspector General section can do these audits internally.

- **Economy and efficiency audits** are management or operational audits. These audits examine a governmental unit's managerial and administrative practices for economy and cost efficiency and strive to identify the cause of any cost inefficiencies (Appendix B).

- **Program audits** or evaluations monitor results to determine the extent to which a governmental unit has achieved program objectives. They also evaluate the cost effectiveness of the alternatives that were employed.

- **Performance audits** review all the operations of a governmental unit and encompass all three types of audits: financial, economy, efficiency, and program results. Performance audits are an increasingly common means of ensuring that those entrusted with management of public services and programs are held accountable.

Regardless of the type of audit or evaluation being conducted, there are three phases to any evaluation process. These involve planning, collecting data, and a final phase of decision making based on findings and recommendations.

The overall objective of any evaluation of various programs and operations is to see if the programs are still relevant or meeting the goals originally established. Besides relevance, there must also be some verification that results are being achieved and that the program is cost effective. In order to perform such an evaluation, data must be collected. Data can be divided into several categories:

- **Quantitative data**—numerical type information;
- **Qualitative data**—observations related to categories, e.g., size, type, color, etc.;
- **Subjective data**—personal perceptions, attitudes, etc. ;
- **Objective data**—observations based on facts (Note: Both objective and subjective data can be either qualitatively or quantitatively measured.);
- **Longitudinal data**—data collected over time;
- **Cross-sectional data**—collected at the same point in time but over different types of agencies, e.g., purchasing volume for schools, municipalities, or counties;
- **Primary data**—collected by the one preparing the evaluation directly from the source; and
- **Secondary data**—collected and recorded by another person or organization (Note: It may have been collected for altogether different purposes and may or may not relate to the particular purpose for which it is it used in a different evaluation.).

Often, the role of monitoring purchasing as well as other programs' performance falls to the internal auditor or Inspector General. They are responsible for ensuring that the policies and procedures are adhered to for the expenditure of goods and services. Procedures employed include reviewing current policies and procedures for compliance. A few files will be selected from the previous year's bid or proposal files. These will be scrutinized for compliance with all procedures. Was the award made in accordance with the ordinances and laws of the agency? Were there any discrepancies in the purchase? These auditors may also use some secondary data from other sources as a comparison to see if best practices are being employed. Benchmarking against other communities can also aid in determining the effectiveness of the various departments and programs of an agency.

If the audit is done in the spirit of trying to improve performance, the final report can usually be used for this purpose. Above all, an audit report needs to be helpful, both for operational managers and for senior management, e.g., one procurement agency was told it needed additional *staffing and* electronic procurement aids. While this agency was not able to get any additional *staffing, it* was able to get funding in the budget for additional computers and software. If audits are conducted with the idea of always finding something wrong or as a political vendetta, then the final audit report may be feared and most surely will report something unexpected. Some agencies have been surprised by reports, which try to lay the blame for problems that are not within their control. One agency was criticized for not following through on contract administration of the various contracts, but the ordinance and procedures under which the agency operated specifically stated procurement was not to be involved. The agency was able to turn this sour report into something useful by expanding procurement's role into the logical extension of following the contract from birth to completion.

Most audits will allow the agency being audited to review the draft report to correct any glaring deficiencies in the data being reported. In addition, most agencies can also prepare a response to the audit report giving any corrective action being pursued or pointing out any inconsistencies in the report.

Based on the results of these various types of audits, department and program budgets may be adjusted. A word of caution must be offered: If a public agency is performing badly, it needs not less money but a change in leadership or at least some improvement in its leadership. Keeping the same management at the agency while giving it fewer resources will hardly improve performance.

Risk Management

*R*isk management is the process of planning, organizing, directing, and controlling the resources and activities of an organization in order to minimize the adverse effects of accidental losses at the least possible cost—the chief objectives of any government. Risk management programs are to preserve the assets of the agency, to assure the continuity of its operations, to assure continued high quality of services, and to maintain safe working conditions. Historically, governmental agencies were less concerned about the problem of risk management because of laws that protected governmental bodies with immunity sanctions from lawsuits. Increasingly, many states do not have so-called governmental immunity laws, and there are many U.S. federal laws which do not provide local agencies with immunity. Additionally, agencies must be prepared to repair and replace structures damaged by natural causes, vandalism or violence.

Agencies have realized the need for professional risk managers—experts who are capable of analyzing the potential risk situation for departments—the insurance needs, and the amount of financial coverage necessary to protect the entire government. Once risks are identified, the agency must decide whether to retain the risk through some form of self-insurance or to avoid the risk. Procurement has a role to work hand-in-hand with risk management. In fact, many risk management divisions report to the procurement director. From elementary things such as the bidding of insurance, which requires some special procedures to accomplish, to knowing the levels of insurance required for service and construction contractors, risk management plays an important role.

There are six steps in risk management:

- identification of exposures;
- evaluation of loss potential;
- selection of a method of loss control;
- implementation;
- monitoring of results; and
- modification of programs based on results.

The identification process involves collecting data on the types of losses an agency might experience. Prior loss histories are available from agency or insurance company records. A review should be made of all property, liability, and personnel losses. Property losses result from damage to various buildings and equipment. Liability losses result from various torts, such as damage caused to others' property, trespass, false arrest/detention, defective products, etc. Personnel losses result from such things as discrimination, hiring, firing, and other issues related to the employment process.

Additional information on the types of losses that might be incurred by an agency is available from budget documents, inquiries of similar agencies, inspections of agency property, and personal interviews of departments. The legislative agenda of the governing body is also a good source of information on the types of activities or actions that may result in future losses.

Once the types of exposures are identified, the agency must determine the chance and magnitude of a potential loss. Once the probability and severity of a loss has been determined, a loss control method can be developed to address the loss. There are two types of risk control mechanisms: avoidance and loss control.

Avoidance involves not doing the particular activity. For example, one agency was going to acquire a shooting range. The primary purpose of the range was for police training. The police department wanted to open the range to the public. An analysis of the risk by the risk management department advised that opening to the public could result in a high probability of claims from the public. A joint decision was made not to open the range to the public.

Loss Control involves both prevention and reduction of losses by such things as safety training, site inspection, quality assurance, and risk mitigation.

- **Risk Retention.** Retention occurs when the agency decides to set aside funds to pay for the loss. Depending on the financial resources available to the agency, it may be determined to pay for the first $500 to $50,000 of any loss. If the agency has a history of sustaining ten property losses of vehicles totaling $10,000 per year, it would be prudent to set aside $10,000 to pay for these losses. Why? Because to purchase insurance for these losses would result in having to pay a premium for insurance, which would probably be more than $10,000. Insurance companies are going to want to cover historical losses as well as cover administrative costs and make a profit. Risk management axiom number one is: *Don't insure losses that are predictable.*

- **Risk Transfer.** The most common type of risk financing involves the purchase of insurance to cover the loss. This may be some form of liability, property, or other type of insurance. It is wise to insure losses, which have a low probability of occurrence but a high severity of damage. As an example, it would be prudent to insure a building for fire losses. Risk management axiom numbers two and three are applicable here:

  Don't risk a lot for a little. If insurance is available at a reasonable cost and the potential loss is large, the choice should be to purchase the insurance. Just because there have been no property losses for 20 years, it is still wise to carry property insurance.

  Don't risk more than you can afford to lose. If the agency has very few resources it should not avoid purchasing insurance unless there are sufficient funds set aside to pay potential losses.

In addition, another type of risk transfer is by contract. Procurement is very familiar with requiring both hold-harmless clauses and requirements for contractors to provide insurance, which will protect the agency from losses caused by the execution of the contract.

Conclusion

*T*his chapter has attempted to introduce the reader to some of the complexities associated with budgeting in the public sector. We first identified some of the major perspectives associated with budgeting, noting that how one sees things impacts what one expects to receive in a budget, i.e. a politician will expect something totally different than, say for example, and accountant. These various perspectives further add to the complexity of budgeting. The politician may see the budget as a tool to determine who wins and who looses in the allocation of organizational resources, while an accountant may see the budget as a legal document that cannot be altered by appointed department heads without approval from the elected officials. Each of the perspectives will require different budget formats—accountants may prefer a line-item budget format while a politician may prefer a program or performance budget format. Both perspectives have their particular strengths and weaknesses, and both are correct in what they expect out of the budget process.

We noted in this chapter that the budget cycle is very similar to the procurement cycle that we identified previously as diving the procurement process. This dovetails well with our contention that procurement must be actively engaged in the budget process if resource allocation decisions are to be made with the most accessible information to make informed decisions. What is just as important to note, is that the different stages of the budget cycle require multi-year budget activities, and that these activities often occur within any given fiscal year. Thus adding to the complexity of public sector budgeting. During each fiscal year the government will be planning for the next budget cycle, acting on the current budget, implementing the current budget, and evaluating previous budgets.

In all, this chapter has provided a glimpse at a very difficult and often confusing budget process. There are a number of books devoted to this subject matter, and students are encouraged to learn as much as possible about budgeting in order to effectuate proper procurement planning and strategic planning in the public sector.

References

Aronson, J. R. (Ed.) (1996). *Management policies in local government finance* (4th ed). Washington, DC: International City/County Management Association.

Behn, R. D. (1994, December). The wrong way to motivate. *Governing*, p. 70.

Behn, R. D. (1995, April). Government needs training too. *Governing*, p. 68.

Bestor, M. (1993, December). Negotiating skills for budget officers. *Government Finance Review*.

Lowi, T. (1969). *The end of liberalism*. New York: W. W. Norton.

Petersen, J. E., & Strachota, D. R. (1991). *Local government finance, concepts and practices*. Chicago, Illinois : Government Finance Officers Association.

Proctor, A. J. (1992, December). New directions in budgeting and fiscal planning. *Government Finance Review*.

Program evaluation methods: Measurement and attribution of program results (3rd ed.). Review Practices and Studies, Government Review and Qualitative Services. Deputy Comptroller General Branch, Treasury Board of Canada Secretariat, Ottawa, Ontario.

Strachota, D. (1994). *The best of governmental budgeting, A guide to preparing budget documents.* Chicago, Illinois: Government Finance Officers Association.

Survey of best practices of comptrollership (1997, July). Consulting and Audit Canada (CAC) reference 5209229.CHAPTER 5

CHAPTER 5

Purchasing Strategies: Their Relationship to Requirements Determination in the Acquisition Process

*R*equirements determination is a key component in the procurement plan-ning process that, if done properly, can result in significant savings for the organization.[1] Unfortunately, due to the reactive nature of government, this critical step is rarely used or, at the very best, under-utilized. Because require-ments determination is based upon analysis of the buying habits of the user and its success necessitates a tracking mechanism, smaller jurisdictions often lack the resources to utilize this valuable component. Even today, many large and small jurisdictions do not have sufficient human and equipment resources to implement sound planning and scheduling programs.

Prior to software programs that provided the capability to analyze orders in terms of quantities, schedules, commodities types, and frequency, the ability of the procurement manager to determine user requirements was virtually non-existent unless the information was tracked manually. In addition, the user had to be a willing participant in the process in order to determine correct quanti-ties and appropriate buying schedules.

Today, even with the ability to extract commodity information to determine appropriate buying plans and schedules, implementing a successful require-

---

[1] For the purpose of this discussion, requirements determination includes analysis of past usage, planning for future usage, reviewing performance, discussion with the user to understand how it is to be used, scheduling, analyzing market conditions, researching alternatives for cost savings, revising quantities and specifications, and discussions with current and potential suppliers.

ments determination program requires a team approach between the buyer and the user.[2] Procurement managers and buyers are challenged to change the attitudes of users determined to protect individual turf so they can maximize value for the organization. Convincing the user to plan and schedule purchases is often a difficult hurdle to overcome when the user is subject to multiple agendas and pressures from elected officials and limited time to accomplish more than the daily tasks.

determining the proper solicitation method...

This chapter discusses requirements determination as the foundation for selection of the best purchase method. It examines the criticality of analyzing commodity usage and customer needs to achieve maximum value in terms of quality level, dollars, and time. Only after requirements are analyzed in terms of quantity, frequency, characteristics, market trends, and needs of the user is the buyer able to identify and proceed with the "best method" to obtain a results-oriented purchase. The relationship between determining requirements as a critical strategy in the procurement process and defining the process and the tools that can be utilized to determine needs is also explored. Assessment of past, current, and future requirements is critical to selecting the most advantageous type of contract and the proper procurement method. If it is not a part of the process, procurement does not achieve the desired results.

This chapter discusses the role of planning and scheduling in determining the proper solicitation method for any procurement. Purchases are dynamic and ever changing; elements and characteristics vary when the commodity remains the same. Market trends and conditions dictate when and how to buy. Existing contracts should be re-evaluated and researched prior to selection of the procurement method to include changes to ensure a correct and value purchase.

The chapter also examines the different methods of procurement and appropriate usage, including variations and hybrids, such as design-build and bridging in competitive sealed bidding. Various strategies that can be utilized in the competitive proposal process to achieve effective results in design and implementation are offered for consideration.

[2]It is important for the purchasing manager to establish a good working relationship with users so that the department provides sufficient information to result in a good or value purchase. The attitude of users who do not understand procurement's role in the organization is that only information provided on the request is necessary. Because of the many demands placed on the user, typically, planning is secondary to immediate need.

Procurement professionals today understand the methods of solicitation and appropriate use of each method. Yet, they sometimes focus on the method only as it relates to what regulations require without taking into consideration what is the best result for the user and the organization. Practitioners are constantly challenged to work within the legal framework to achieve value by selection of the best method, based upon the requirements of the user. All factors should be taken into consideration, including time, quality level, cost, availability of product or service, competition, specifications, market trends and present and future usage.

Defining Customer Needs

Requirements determination has traditionally been recognized as one of the initial steps in the procurement planning cycle (see Chapter 2). The *Advanced Public Procurement* (2001) textbook published by the National Institute of Governmental Purchasing, Inc., identified functions in the cycle to include:

- coordinating with user agencies;
- recognition of the need;
- description of the need;
- budget analysis;
- creation of market studies for important materials; and
- discussion with sales representatives.

These functions and their impact on the procurement process are discussed throughout this chapter.

As noted in previous chapters, historically, procurement has not been involved in the initial stages of government planning. Its role has been to obtain the goods and services in a timely manner at the most economical cost. Generally, procurement is not notified until a customer "recognizes a need" and prepares a request to purchase.

If the procurement function is to be truly effective in maximizing value, staff needs to be involved up front, in both capital and operating budgetary processes. Initial involvement alerts procurement management of operating requirements and capital equipment purchases for upcoming and future years so that staff can research market trends and determine appropriate buying schedules.

Not knowing requirements until receipt of a requisition automatically places the procurement function into a reactive mode. The user's requested delivery is usually short, and the need is often immediate. As a result, procurement staff barely has sufficient lead time to research and prepare solicitations for one-time purchases or implementation of a term contract. Depending on the dollar amount and the type of procurement, the process can take several days to several months.

This process discourages planning and scheduling—the two critical components of strategic procurement planning. A better solution is for procurement managers to be involved in the government's strategic planning and budgetary process. In this staff or advisory role, Procurement becomes a key player in planning by researching to ensure that materials, products and services are available, time lines are met, and delays are minimized (NIGP, 1999 pp. 9-12). With their knowledge of market conditions, procurement managers can forecast more accurate costs and determine realistic schedules for upcoming programs and projects.

Budget Process Models

*T*he following represents a comparison of the governmental budget process. The traditional model does not include procurement in the process until after the budget has been requested by users, reviewed by financial staff and budget committee, approved by the governing body, and implemented. Because procurement has no input into scheduling purchases, there are impacts on price and lead time. Market conditions cannot be analyzed until a request is submitted to staff.

The second model is preferred, because it shows procurement involvement in the budget process. At the approval stage of the budget, procurement staff is already aware of requests. Under this scenario, procurement researches the product or service at the point when the user is anticipating the need in conjunction with the budget development process. Staff has sufficient time to determine if items should be bought on an annual or seasonal basis, whether there is a long or short lead time, or if there is a shortage in the market. There is also time to research possible alternate and equivalent products.

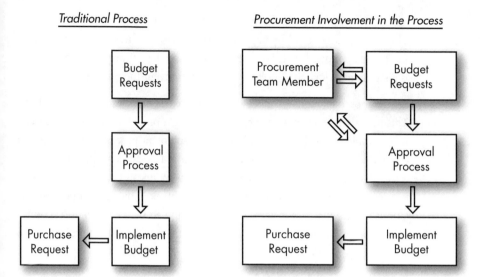

Figure 20 - *Budget process models.*

Successful completion of this initial step results in maximum value for the government. In order to meet this goal, it is critical that Procurement coordinates closely with its internal customers, develop supplier relations, and understand market conditions. Step one occurs when the user department determines need and submits a request that accurately portrays required quantity, description of the item or service, and delivery. This should be provided within a planning framework that allows procurement staff sufficient time to research possible cost-saving alternatives and analyze previous purchases in terms of successes and failures, requirements changes, and vendor and product performance.

Procurement staff should review previous purchases carefully and compare them to current requests. Users, often in their haste to submit a request to purchase, fail to update specifications, which result in a muddled process, incorrect information, and unnecessary addenda. Once the information has been verified, the buyer should examine market conditions to determine lead time, availability, and possible alternatives that may result in cost savings. To do this successfully, buyers must analyze, research, and question so that they understand what they are buying.

One of the biggest frustrations user departments have with the procurement process is the tendency of buyers to handle a purchase request without understanding how the item or service will be utilized. This is a critical component of recognition of need. Perhaps, more than anything else, "buying blind" causes users to label procurement as "buying a low bid" product or service that is not the required quality level and does not perform to expected standards. The result is a waste of taxpayer dollars, because the item is rarely or never used or is even discarded. The user may develop the attitude that procurement is a stumbling block and look for way to circumvent the process.

Buyers should take time to talk to their users about new or unfamiliar requests. This may require a visit to a site or researching a program. The up-front work saves problems on the back end of the procurement process when it is often too late to make corrections. At this point, a bid or proposal may have to be rejected, extended, or cancelled to correct misunderstandings. If the purchase is delayed, procurement becomes a stumbling block. If bid and proposal solicitations require that all vendor questions be handled by the buyer and prohibit discussions with the user during the process, then one should logically assume that the buyer understands the procurement.

Recognition of need also involves analysis of data. Procurement software systems are continually improving, and the majority today provide historical data for quantities and types of commodity purchases, order frequency, usage, and price. The ability to produce a procurement profile and analyze past purchases is invaluable to buyers to determine and schedule future purchases, clarify specifications, and expedite the process.

Requirements analysis examines specifications to eliminate products and services that are not cost effective and do not result in value. Value is measured in terms of suitability and cost. This is defined in public sector procurement as the lowest cost to meet a need, where need is defined as quality that performs at an acceptable level. It invites change and looks for better ways to accomplish a given task. Users are encouraged to suggest products and services that should be analyzed, including high annual dollar purchases, large volume/quantity purchases, and items that lend themselves to standardization—what was labeled Quadrant IV procurements.

Buying Plan and Analysis Methods

Once a strategic plan has been developed and a budget has been established for the coming year, a precise buying plan should be developed for the same time period. A buying plan based on various types of analyses should be developed for each major material or category of materials. In order to develop a buying plan, the purchasing professional must be aware of the nature of volume and timing decisions.

The first variable to be considered in volume and timing decisions is the stability of the market. Materials that are produced in stable markets are basically standard off-the-shelf supply items. In a reasonably competitive economy, forces of supply and demand determine the price level at which the standard products will be sold. This may be true in the long run. In the short run, however, the only way a buyer can influence the price he or she pays for these items is through some type of volume buying arrangement that affords the supplier the means of reducing costs.

Unstable markets are those that exhibit short-run fluctuation. Typical of these types of commodities are oil and petroleum-based products, paper, crude rubber, and many types of metals. Many of these commodities have their price determined by international political situations, weather, growing conditions, and speculation as well as supply and demand considerations. In unstable markets, timing becomes an important consideration.

Buyers are interested in ensuring that their organizations have an adequate supply of commodities. In a market with price stability, timing is not as critical as it is in an unstable market. Careful observation and analysis of market conditions are essential, as buyers hope to satisfy their price and supply objectives. Although buyers cannot control the market price, they can, by careful timing of their purchases, control to some extent the price they pay.

The buying plan consists of analysis of demand, market, and supplier. The first is demand analysis, which is used to estimate annual requirements based on the previous year plus anticipated use for the upcoming year. Demand analysis utilizes the "ABC" system based on the Pareto principle that categorizes materials into classifications based on percentages. Applying the Pareto model, 80% of purchase dollars are expended on 20% of supply quantity. The 80% is further categorized by ABC classification where *A* represents 70% of materials need, *B* represents 20%, and *C* represents 10%. A plan is developed for each group that is used to determine usage based on demand.

The second analysis is based on market assessment, which involves researching product availability, market volatility, supply and demand, and price. This should be a continuous process so that buying schedules can be adjusted to achieve maximum availability and the best price. When a commodity is high cost and difficult to obtain, buyers should spot buy on an as-needed basis. Suppliers are usually not able to enter into long-term contracts and maintain fixed pricing. If they are forced to enter into a long-term contract, they will usually inflate pricing to insure against losses. On the other hand, when commodities are readily available and price is low, buyers should implement term contracts with fixed pricing and escalation/de-escalation clauses for price increases and decreases.

The third type is supplier analysis, which determines the availability of competition and the possibility of more economical or effective alternative products. Assessing performance of a current supplier falls into this category of analysis. Purchasing professionals should have documented both good and poor performance to determine if the supplier meets the standard for an acceptable vendor. This type of analysis should be ongoing, as it represents a critical step to achieve maximum value for the government.

Value Analysis

Value analysis or value engineering (interchangeable terms) is an organized effort to analyze the function of systems, products, specifications, standards, practices, and procedures in order to satisfy the required function most economically (National Association of State Procurement Officials, 2001 pp. 34). A successful value analysis/ engineering program supported by top management will result in lower costs or more effective means of delivering services to the taxpayer.

Value analysis employs techniques that identify the functions the user requires from a product or service. It establishes by comparison the appropriate cost for each function, but it requires knowledge, creativity, and initiative to find alternate approaches to provide each function at the appropriate cost. Value analysis is strictly a team effort. Purchasing must constructively question user agency needs, requests, and specifications. The user agencies must, in turn, question purchasing practices, such as source selection and award decisions based on price.

Value analysis is strictly a team effort.

To fully understand the concept of value analysis, we must first define "value." Value can be defined as the lowest end cost at which the function can be accomplished at the same time and place and with the quality required. Value cannot be determined exclusively by examination of the item under review. The value of any service, material, or product is established by the minimum costs of other available alternatives, materials, products, or services that will perform the same function.

Most organizations establish cross-functional teams when they wish to carry out the value analysis process. A workshop method encourages free discussion and exchange of ideas among the team members. The team members should be selected on the basis of their knowledge and ability to contribute to the organization's strategies. Of course, purchasing and the user agencies should be part of this team. This team can also serve as an evaluation and negotiation team during the solicitation and award phase of the contract.

Since value analysis is based on a systematic approach to acquiring the basic function at the lowest cost, it cannot be emphasized too strongly that the logical sequence and applications of the techniques and the job plan must be followed in order to obtain the benefits desired. Following this approach will enable the team to:

- accumulate facts;
- identify areas of knowledge required;
- provide an efficient knowledge search;
- apply creative skills; and
- apply precise evaluation techniques.

Forecasting

*F*orecasting is a tool to determine future needs. It should be an ongoing assessment to examine opportunities and is an essential element of strategic planning. It requires procurement professionals to keep abreast of the market and surveys and understand various indicators, business cycles, indexes, lead times, and price histories of commodities and services. Forecasting should be used to determine the type of solicitation, such as a spot bid or term contract, based upon market fluctuations and conditions.

A particularly important index for procurement is the Purchasing Manager's Index (PMI). The PMI is a well-established and reliable indicator that identifies highs and lows in the economy. It provides an indication of what will occur in the future, based upon past trends. Other important indicators that procurement professionals should be familiar with include new orders, production, employment, supplier deliveries, and inventories. Indexes are categorized as diffusion indexes, where they measure change in economic and business activity.

Forecasting is a plan that requires knowledge of the economy. In order to predict what will occur in the future, examination of current and past trends and pricing is critical. When the procurement professional is involved up front in the initial planning and budgeting processes, there is adequate time to forecast to buy effectively, make good decisions, and maximize value.

Spot Bids

Spot bids are defined as "a one-time purchase occasioned by a small requirement, an unusual or emergency circumstance, or a favorable market condition" (NIGP, 2001). When requirements cannot be forecasted with accuracy, during emergencies as well as volatile market conditions, spot market purchases are required. Public purchasers need to pay particular attention to fluctuations in the market such that their knowledge of the ins and outs of the marketplace benefit their agency. As an example, a buyer's forecast of liquid petroleum gas usage could reap the agency significant savings when purchased off-season and stored for delivery during high-demand periods when prices escalate dramatically. Timing of these purchases can generate substantial savings when buyers have analyzed a commodity and know when the conditions are favorable for greatest economy.

Term Contracts

Historical data forms the basis for term, or requirements, contracts. If commodities such as asphalt, concrete, uniforms, janitorial products, and office supplies are purchased in large quantities and repetitively, there is justification for a contract. Term contracting, broadly defined, is a procurement technique that establishes a source of supply for deliveries or services to be made over a period of time (NIGP, 1996). There are a number of possible arrangements: definite quantity for a definite period, definite quantity for an indefinite period, indefinite quantity for a definitive period, and indefinite quantity for an indefinite period. They are typically structured on a quarterly, six-month, annually or multi-year basis, depending upon the volatility of price and the ability of the vendor to deliver for an extended period. Term contracts, because of the volume, generally result in lower prices and administrative efficiency.

Once a term contract is executed, user departments often have the capability to purchase directly from contracts without having to make a request through the procurement office. If there is a computerized financial program to track usage when departments place direct orders, then the basis is formed for the subsequent bid and a more accurate contract.

Research should also include the feasibility of demand contracts compared to warehousing an item. An example of a value stockless inventory contract is office supplies that can be ordered and delivered directly from the vendor within a short time frame. Instead of warehousing supplies that can be lost to spoilage, deterioration, or user preference, orders are placed from the supply catalog where price is based upon a percentage discount from the list. An additional benefit is that once the contract is established user departments can place orders without having to make a request through the procurement office.

Inventory Forecasting

A key function of inventory management is forecasting the anticipated need for various commodities. Forecasting is usually done by taking historical data and making an analysis to determine if any changes in future requirements are anticipated. The most frequently used means of forecasting future usage are based upon various methods of averaging past usage. These analysis methods include fixed period average, moving average, and weighted average.

Fixed Period Method

The fixed period method divides the total usage for a fixed period of time (e.g., the last calendar or fiscal year) by the number of months involved. The resulting monthly average figure is the forecast for the entire comparable future period. For example, if 1,200 units are used during either a calendar year of January 1 through December 31 or a fiscal year beginning July 1, average monthly usage can be projected at 100 units. The time period selected must always remain the same in order to compare usage patterns properly. Although this method is very simple to use in forecasting future trends, care must be taken because it may well reflect old trends and not the most current experience.

Moving Average Method

The moving average method always uses current data from the immediate past period. For example, forecasts for an annual or fiscal year would incorporate data from the immediately preceding twelve months. (Projections in January incorporate information from the previous January through December, projections in February would incorporate information from February of the preceding year through the end of January, etc.) As the year progresses, the average is updated by dropping the oldest month's data and adding the most recent month's data. This is a far more accurate means of making projections than the fixed period method.

Weighted Moving Average Method

The weighted moving average method builds even more accuracy into the system by giving more significance to weighting specific information such as seasonal variations. (For example, more heating oil is used in the winter.) In such a case, special consideration is given to those months in which usage is higher, and they will be given a higher weight in determining annual forecasts.

Regardless of the method used, historically based forecasts are not always accurate. Averages reflect a mathematical calculation of a series of numbers. For example, the average of 13 and 1 and 8 and 6 is 7 in both cases, but the average of 7 obtained from the 8 and 6 values is more dependable because of the larger variance between 13 and 1. The difference from the average to the sample value is called the Mean Absolute Deviation (MAD). In determining the amount of inventory to keep on hand, we must consider the mean absolute deviation as well as the average. The formula to calculate MAD is:

$$MAD = \frac{ABSOLUTE\ VALUE\ OF\ ERRORS}{NUMBER\ OF\ ERRORS}$$

In the above examples, the MAD would be 6 in one case and 1 in the other. There are mathematical formulas available for using this and other information, such as safety factors and lead times, to determine the proper re-ordering points in an inventory management program. Traditionally, ordering quantity is the amount of material required during lead time plus a safety stock based in part on the MAD calculation.

Economic Ordering Quantity (EOQ)

Despite a trend toward stockless purchasing and just-in-time purchasing systems, inventories are still very much a reality in day-to-day operations. Normally, user departments advocate the maintenance of high inventories, and the purchasing department advocates lower inventories to minimize cost. Carrying material in inventory is expensive.

Two basic categories of costs are associated with inventories: carrying costs and acquisition costs. Carrying costs represent the costs of maintaining the inventory, including the cost of invested funds, insurance, storage, obsolescence and deterioration, equipment, and labor. The carrying cost is defined by the following formula:

(carrying cost/year) = (average inventory value) x

(inventory carrying cost expressed as a percentage of inventory value)

Acquisition costs are those costs involved in making a purchase. Many jurisdictions indicate that the cost of issuing a purchase order may be in the range of $100.00 to $150.00. The formula for determining acquisition costs is the following:

(acquisition cost /year) =

(number of orders placed / year) x (acquisition cost per order)

If we examine the above, it becomes apparent that the more times a year we order, the lower our inventory costs become. However, the more times we order, the higher our acquisition costs. The total cost to the organization for material acquisition and inventory maintenance is the sum of these costs. Purchasing is always striving to minimize these costs. Minimum overall cost is achieved with Economic Ordering Quantity (EOQ) that is expressed in both dollars and units, according to the following formulas.

$$\text{EOQ in \$} = \sqrt{\frac{2 \times (\text{annual requirements in \$}) \times (\text{ordering cost per order in \$})}{\text{Carrying cost as percentage}}}$$

$$\text{EOQ in units} = \sqrt{\frac{2 \times (\text{annual usage in units}) \times (\text{acquisition cost in \$ per order})}{(\text{Delivered unit cost in \$}) \times (\text{inventory carrying cost as percentage})}}$$

Table 3 illustrates an example of EOQ using the following assumptions:

- Total annual usage = $12,000 ($1,000 per month);
- Delivered Unit Cost = $1;
- Acquisition Cost (cost per purchase order) = $125.00;
- Average Inventory Value = 50% of Purchase Amount; and
- Carrying Costs = 30% of Inventory Value

Table 3

Economic Ordering Quanity

	Number of Orders per Year					
	1	2	3	4	6	12
$ per order	12,000	6,000	4,000	3,000	2,000	1,000
Average Inventory Value (50%)	6,000	3,000	2,000	1,500	1,000	500
Carrying Costs (30%)	1,800	900	600	450	300	150
Acquisition Cost ($125 per P.O.)	125	250	375	500	750	1,500
Total Cost = Acquisition + Carrying	1,925	1,150	975	950	1,050	1,650

Using the simple example above, it is apparent from the table that the least costly alternative is buying four (4) times a year, with 3,000 units per order. Both EOQ formulas yield the same result—the most economic order quantity is 3,162 units ($3,162 dollars per order), which translates to four orders per year.

Determining the Method of Solicitation

Selection of the solicitation method occurs after the buyer has analyzed requirements to determine if the purchase should be combined into a repetitive on-demand type contract on a one-time, as-needed basis. While it is good customer service to include the user in the process, Procurement must have final decision authority for the solicitation method. Procurement staff has the expertise to determine the best method to achieve the most cost-effective results, including emergency, single, or sole source items that are normally outside a competitive process.

The public sector sets definite parameters in legislation where dollar limits or conditions typically establish the ground rules for the solicitation. For example, governments may set a competitive sealed bid requirement for all materials and equipment at specific dollar amounts, ranging from as low as $1,000 up to $100,000. The basis for award is the lowest price, provided the bidder is responsible and has submitted a responsive bid. The competitive sealed proposal method is generally used when price is not the determining factor and would not result in the best value. Usually the procurement involves a service or where clear specifications are not available.

Generally, there is flexibility in how a purchase can be handled below the bid threshold. Small dollar purchases require competition, and emergency and sole source purchases require user justification; however, the buyer has latitude regarding the solicitation process. Buyers need to be cognizant of the fact that the small dollar purchase can be as complex and time-consuming as the larger dollar purchase. Non-competitive purchases, such as sole source and emergency purchases, have the potential to cause problems in the procurement process and tarnish a buyer's credibility, if not carefully researched and documented.

Assessment of Market Conditions

*A*n assessment of the market reveals current price and fluctuations as well as product shortages or surpluses. This step is critical to the planning process; for, without it, the buyer risks the opportunity to achieve value. Buying when prices are high or the product is in short demand results in over-payment. Either of these conditions requires delaying the purchase or decreasing the quantity until the market is less volatile. A one-time purchase only as needed prevents spending excessive dollars.

Conversely, a buyer should purchase a greater quantity when prices are low and the product is in large supply. There are obvious conditions that should be present, such as when the organization's usage for the product is high and ongoing, sufficient warehouse space is available, and the item's shelf life is sufficiently long to avoid spoilage or deterioration.

The skilled purchasing manager utilizes all publications, monthly and quarterly indexes, and current product updates to analyze market conditions and determine the best time to buy. Based on market conditions, the buyer is able to select a formal bid, negotiation, or small purchase method that results in the best value. It is incumbent upon the purchasing manager to regularly survey conditions to determine the appropriate purchasing method.

An assessment of the market should include discussion with suppliers. A good relationship with these individuals is one of the greatest resources available to the procurement professional to gain knowledge of market conditions, product information, and an awareness of competition. In the past, public sector procurement tended to avoid association with suppliers based upon a narrow interpretation of competitive requirements and the desire to avoid any sign of favoritism for one supplier over another. Government procurement officials have since learned the importance of partnering with suppliers and developed practices to utilize their expertise without compromising integrity. Implementing term contracts with optional renewals is one mechanism to achieve the longer-term relationship.

Determining the Method of Solicitation Based on Requirements Analysis

*T*he importance of researching and analyzing requests cannot be over-emphasized. These techniques separate a value from a non-value procurement. The procurement professional should strive for excellence by utilizing these techniques to build trust and confidence with the requestor and credibility for the department.

This section discusses the different purchasing methods and the impact that requirements determination has on each of them. Failure to include this step has the capability to cause problems in the solicitation, award, and contract administration processes. Correct information is critical for a successful purchase.

Competitive Quotations and Competitive Sealed Bids

While quotations and bids are based on similar principles and follow similar processes, they differ in complexity, amount of time involved, and structure. Both solicitation methods are price motivated, which serves as the basis for award provided the requirements for responsiveness and responsibility are met. Responsiveness refers to the bid meeting requirements and specifications. Responsibility refers to the bidder having the capability of performing the work or delivering the product/equipment in terms of past performance, financial capability, experience, references, etc. Both methods require extensive research and analysis to determine correct specifications, quantity usage, and vendor selection based upon performance.

An example of the use of requirements determination for a competitive quotation for landscaping plants would include the following steps: checking the request to ensure all information has been included by the user department; understanding the purpose and location of where the plants will be used; talking with the user to see if the plants are going to be needed on a recurring basis; analyzing market conditions, availability, and pricing; researching alternatives that may be more cost effective; and checking the performance of vendors who have supplied plants in the past. These steps provide the buyer with information for both current and future planning and scheduling. If plants are to be purchased on a recurring basis, the buyer may consider a term contract. When price fluctuates, the buyer utilizes spot or as-needed purchases to achieve greater value. If prices spike at certain times of the year or if plants are seasonal, then the buyer looks at scheduled buying. If the buyer is procuring specialty plants, it may require ordering in advance of seeding to allow the contractor sufficient time to order and receive the seeds versus purchasing stock from a nursery.

A critical component of requirements determination in the acquisition process is selection of suppliers. Vendors with poor performance should not be included in the solicitation process. A good procurement department maintains a current file on performance.

The process is similar for the competitive sealed bid, only more complex with several additional steps. Primarily driven by dollar limits that require sealed bidding, there are other criteria required in the process. Bids are publicly advertised, usually from two to four weeks, depending upon the jurisdiction's legal requirements. There must be clear specifications and adequate available competition. Price is the determining factor based on responsiveness to the specifications. Bid responses are sealed, kept in a secure location, and publicly opened on a specified date and time. Discussion with bidders is not allowed except for clarification.

The competitive sealed bid process is a lengthy process, and extra time should be built into the planning phase. For example, many governments require a longer advertising period for public work projects. This becomes critical where there is a construction project or a renovation project that requires an on-site pre-bid conference. Out-of-town bidders often need additional time for travel arrangements in order to attend pre-bid conferences. The buyer should analyze the complexity of the purchase and include sufficient time to issue addenda.

Requirements determination plays an important role in determining the best bid method for construction of facilities. An opportunity to achieve value and savings in both dollars and time occurs when the procurement director participates in the budget process. The user department and procurement director work together to determine whether a project should be constructed by the traditional design-bid-build, design-build, bridging, design-build-finance-operate-maintain, or design-build-operate-maintain procurement method (American Bar Association, 2000). The ability to use these hybrids of the traditional design-bid-build procurement method provides an opportunity to reduce administrative and construction time. Understanding that the needs of the jurisdiction is a key element in order for procurement to be an effective player is best achieved by allowing its participation in the initial planning stages.

Competitive Sealed Proposals

Planning is a critical component for a successful competitive sealed proposal. Step one includes an in-depth evaluation of the procurement request to determine if the proposal method will realize greater value. A buyer should be cognizant of a user's preference for a proposal, which has subjectivity built into the process, over the more objective competitive bid process. A request for a service does not automatically mean that a proposal should be used. The key is the need for evaluation to be based upon criteria rather than price and the absence of clear specifications.

The competitive sealed proposal process is generally complex and lengthy. Many of the same steps in competitive bidding are part of the proposal process, including public advertising, security until opening, and a pre-proposal conference. The process may also include interviews with offerors who are short-listed, then negotiating price with the highest ranked of the selected group. Buyers should include adequate time for these steps to avoid delays in projects or services when they plan and schedule the procurement.

Understanding strategy and what the user needs to accomplish is an important requirements determination step when establishing evaluation criteria for proposals. Consulting firms that regularly provide service to a government have a thorough knowledge of its needs and preferences and may be able to manipulate the evaluation process in their responses. To prevent this, the buyer determines appropriate evaluation criteria. Assigning point value, listing categories without points, and using a multi-step process that combines the proposal and bid processes are techniques that ensure a fair and advantageous award.

Sole Source

Negotiation should be used in a sole source purchase, when it is not advantageous to purchase competitively. Procurement has the responsibility to determine if there is only one product, equipment, or service that can meet the user's requirements or if the item requested needs to be purchased sole source for compatibility with existing equipment. It is important that the user adequately justify a sole source need and that the buyer is comfortable with the justification.

Government purchasing officials may bid a request that should be handled as a sole source, knowing that the specifications are so restrictive that only one response will be received. They erroneously justify this action—that the requirements for competition have been met—because a bid has been issued. There is, however, a difference between a single response bid and a sole source. A single response bid is very often the result of poor selection of bidders, restrictive or unclear specifications, market conditions, or poor scheduling. In some cases, the vendor knows that there will only be one response and does not offer competitive pricing. A single response bid may be awarded if the buyer's research indicates that the process was fair and the award results in value. However, in the public sector, the award may be viewed as suspect and an attempt to avoid the competitive process. Generally, there rarely is value in these bids, as they require additional procurement time to research and re-bid. Buyers should investigate reasons for the one response so that corrective measures can be taken.

A sole source purchase should be negotiated with the vendor. When sole source has been selected as the method of procurement, the next step for the buyer is to carefully plan strategy and objectives to achieve maximum results and value. The buyer should be careful that the user includes reasons for sole source that are not a preference for particular equipment or products. Examples of justifiable sole source include: compatibility with existing equipment or system, parts for repair, proprietary equipment or products, specialized features that are essential to obtain a desired result, compatibility due to training requirements, and testing standards.

Small Dollar Purchases

As previously noted, the analysis of spend via small purchases can be as complex and time-consuming as the larger dollar competitive sealed bid or competitive sealed proposal and should be given as much attention as those that require public advertising and opening. Suppliers often allege that specifications are restrictive to allow preference for a particular product and, because the process does not require public advertising, buyers can select their favorite vendors to submit quotations. There are usually a minimum number of quotations required for the small purchase; and many buyers, instead of pursuing alternate product possibilities, select the vendors they know carry the specified item.

The small purchase request typically has a short delivery time. This, plus the large number of small dollar requests a buyer may process, often result in not thoroughly researching the request. The user may split requirements on two separate requisitions to circumvent the bid process. Even if the buyer does not realize this until after the request has been processed, it still provides information that can be utilized for the next purchase to determine if a term contract, better planning, or schedule buying is appropriate.

Requirements determination in analyzing the small purchase is as critical as in the larger purchase. The request should be researched to determine the best procurement method that results in the greatest value. It cannot be overstated that the buyer should know what is being purchased and how it is going to be used. Questions the buyer should ask include: Can an alternate be used that is available on an existing contract? Is the request a seasonal item that should be placed on a schedule for future purchases? Is the user requesting the item frequently and combining purchases that could provide justification for a demand contract? Should the item be purchased locally for service needs? Is there only one source? Is there a long delivery time? Should more than the required minimum number of quotations be solicited for greater competition and value? How do you select vendors?

know what is being purchased and how it is going to be used.

Planning a small purchase is critical to maximizing value. Using the supply-positioning matrix, as a general rule the small purchases represent 20% of the dollars and 80% of the work volume. Careful analysis can reveal a better way to handle a purchase than a single purchase that results in better service to the user and greater value to the government.

Contract Selection

Requirements determination should play a key role in selection of the type of contract. There are several types of contracts, including the purchase order, firm fixed price, escalation/de-escalation, and cost reimbursable, to name a few. Choosing the wrong type can result in problems in the contract management process. It is imperative that the buyer understands types of contracts and their appropriate use, contract terms and conditions, and works with the user department to determine what will best protect the jurisdiction.

Closely aligned with contract selection is whether to require performance and payment bonds. While bonding requirements are usually dictated by procurement regulations, occasionally there are instances where waiving requirements may be appropriate. An understanding of what is to be accomplished, market conditions, and the profile of contractors who will submit bids or proposals is essential to provide protection and value.

Conclusion

A results-based oriented value-adding procurement does not occur without planning. It involves careful analysis of the past and present and forecasting into the future. The skilled procurement professional evaluates each request and the impact it will have on the organization. The goal is to achieve maximum value and service.

Omission of any of the planning steps can result in problems in evaluation, award and contract administration. Figure 21 summarizes the planning steps discussed in this chapter.

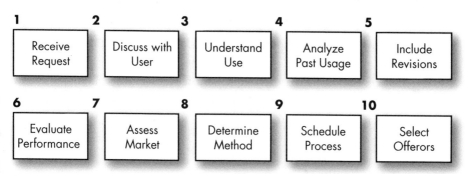

Figure 21 - *Steps in the planning/scheduling process.*

Explanation of Steps:

Receive Request: Procurement receives a purchase request from the user. Buyer checks information for accuracy, including delivery address, required delivery date, complete specifications, etc.

Discuss with User: Buyer discusses request with user to clarify specifications and ensure information is correct.

Understand Use: The solicitation should not be issued until the buyer understands the use. This may involve discussions with the user and a site visit.

Analyze Past Usage: Buyer researches past purchases to identify potential vendors and evaluates quantity usage.

Include Revisions: Buyer incorporates changes after discussion with the user. Evaluation of usage may require adjustments to initial quantity request.

Evaluate Performance: Buyer researches past purchases to identify product or vendor performance problems.

Assess Market: Buyer researches market conditions and analyzes current price and recent history, then determines appropriate quantity, schedule, and type of purchase method.

Determine Purchase Method: Buyer determines purchase method that results in the best value. The jurisdiction's bid requirements and regulations for procurement are the primary consideration.

Schedule Process: Buyer and user work together to schedule a time line depending upon the type of purchase, including: preparing solicitation, advertising, and pre-bid/pre-proposal conferences; evaluation; award; and pre-contract administration meetings.

Select Offerors: Buyer selects specific offerors based upon past performance in addition to those who may respond through advertising.

Planning has been traditionally viewed as a responsibility that occurs when there is extra time. Unfortunately, this rarely occurs in the procurement profession. The purchaser today must be a researcher to be effective and add value. To overcome the clerical stigma, the procurement director should hire professionals who have the ability to question, analyze, and seek better ways to provide for the organization.

References

American Bar Association (2000). Source selection and contract formation (Article 3) and Procurement of infrastructure facilities and services (Article 5). In *The 2000 Model Procurement Code for State and Local Governments* (pp. 22-30, 39-49). Washington, DC: American Bar Association.

Ellram, L. M., & Birou, L. M. (1995). *Purchasing for bottom line impact: Improving the organization through strategic procurement* (Vol. 4, pp. 9-12). Tempe, AZ: National Association of Purchasing Management.

Fearon, H. E., Dobler, D. W., & Killen, K. H. (1993). Management responsibilities and strategies. In *The purchasing handbook* (5th ed., Part 3, pp. 437-494). New York: National Association of Purchasing Management, McGraw Hill.

The National Association of State Procurement Officials (NASPO) (2001). Planning and scheduling. In *State & local government purchasing principles & practices* (Chapter 4, pp. 30-36). Lexington, KY: NASPO.

National Institute of Governmental Purchasing, Inc. (NIGP) (1996). *Dictionary of purchasing terms* (5th ed.). Herndon, VA: NIGP.

National Institute of Governmental Purchasing, Inc. (NIGP) (1999). General principles, objectives and policies. In *General public procurement* (Chapter 1, pp. 9-12). Herndon, VA: NIGP.

National Institute of Governmental Purchasing, Inc. (NIGP) (1999). *Intermediate public procurement*. Herndon, VA: NIGP.

National Institute of Governmental Purchasing, Inc. (NIGP) (2001). Procurement planning and research. In *Advanced public procurement* (Chapter 3, pp. 105-144). Herndon, VA: NIGP.

CHAPTER 6

Specifications

*T*he average procurement official underutilizes the art of specification development and writing. The reason is not because of lack of knowledge or skill but because it is a process that takes research and time. Unfortunately, the procurement official does not always have sufficient time due to pressure from the user to purchase a requested item quickly. Specifications have been described as the "lifeblood of the procurement process," yet they are often neglected (National Association of State Procurement Officials, 2001 p. 44).

Similar to requirements determination, well developed specifications result in savings for the jurisdiction. Poor specification development often causes misunderstandings between the purchaser and user and the purchaser and vendor. This results in poor buying or a more sophisticated product for the intended use, restrictive conditions, and a loss of value to the government.

Specification development builds upon requirements determination by incorporating its essential components. The quantity, quality level, scheduled delivery, and conditions begin as requirements that are then incorporated as specifications into the solicitation document. A successful process occurs only when the user and the buyer work together.

Specification management can significantly impact the specification process. Typically, only the large procurement department, such as a state province, large city, or county, has responsibility for writing specifications. The more common practice is for specifications to be written by the user and then forwarded to the procurement office for review. In this scenario, the buyer's responsibility is to ensure that specifications are nonrestrictive and in collaboration with the user to ensure that the quality level is neither too high nor too low for intended use.

There is always potential for conflict, if the buyer suggests that the specification should be changed. Conflict resolution, teamwork, planning, and research are critical to achieving procurement value. These elements are part of the specification process, just as in the requirements determination, or planning process. This chapter examines how the procurement official can successfully manage the specifications process to achieve value for the organization. Critical to the success of this function is the evolvement of good relationships, whether the user writes and procurement staff reviews or the buyer researches and writes the specifications. Specifications include a discussion of the purpose, importance, and requirements of the specification and its content and may serve different purposes in the private and public sectors based upon the philosophical difference between the two sectors.

The chapter discusses the different types of specifications and their appropriate use, focusing on how to determine what is a good specification and what type of specification results in the greatest value. The skilled procurement professional recognizes that achievement of a smooth and value-added purchase results from knowing the needs of the user and the quality level required for the intended use of the product. Understanding the difference between performance and design specifications and appropriate usage, the type of standard that best protects the organization, where to find sources and help, and how to write clear and concise specifications for solicitations are other considerations. Finally, the chapter defines common technical terms and standards and provides the conventional outline for a purchase description. An objective is to familiarize the student with specification writing principles and techniques that are critical to a buyer's credibility.

Specification Management

*T*he procurement function should have final authority for specifications, even when responsibility for development is housed with the user department. This is particularly important in the public sector where a primary objective is to achieve competition. Unlike the private sector where selection of a vendor does not necessarily follow a competitive process and emphasis is placed on service and performance, governments are required to allow an open process where the underlying principle is based upon qualified suppliers having an equal chance to compete. One of procurement's primary responsibilities is to ensure this, and specifications are a tool to guarantee an equity process by being non-restrictive, capable of being met by two or more suppliers, and allowing for a competitive bid (NIGP, 1999).

Authority for specifications is specifically enumerated in *The 2000 Model Procurement Code for State and Local Governments* (2000). The Code empowers the Chief Procurement Officer to monitor the use of specifications to assure competition, enforce non-restrictive clauses except in appropriate situations, and promote economy for the intended purpose. The Code authorizes the Chief Procurement Officer to obtain advice and assistance from users in specification development and delegate authority to write specifications (American Bar Association, 2000). Delegation falls under the purview of procurement where the buyer has final authority and responsibility for content in the actual solicitation. According to *The 2000 Model Procurement Code,* "all specifications shall seek to promote overall economy for the purposes intended and encourage competition in satisfying the (government's) needs, and shall not be unduly restrictive" (p. 38).

The Code empowers

Jurisdictions often have decentralized specification management due to lack of staff, historical practice, or weak support from top officials for centralized procurement. Decentralization differs from delegation by shifting authority for specification management from the Chief Procurement Officer to the user department. One of the greatest threats is a purchase based upon preference for a particular product. The user wants the best product or equipment that will get the job accomplished, based upon personal experience. If the user lacks knowledge of the procurement function and its principles, then there is conflict when procurement attempts to open restrictive specifications or suggests possible cost-saving alternatives. To ensure competition in the process and avoid conflict, procurement officials should train their users so that they understand principles and legal requirements and why competition, integrity, and equity are critical components of public sector purchasing.

Placing specification management authority within procurement does not minimize the importance or the role of the user department in specification writing. The user has technical expertise and should have significant input into the development of specifications. Specifications should never be developed without the user department's contribution. It takes both parties to realize value by developing specifications at the proper quality level for intended use. While procurement's responsibilities include insuring specifications are nonrestrictive, can be met by at least two competitors, and allowing alternatives that result in value, staff has responsibility to provide sufficient justification and documentation when the government's best interest is realized by a noncompetitive process, specifically sole source, direct negotiation, or emergency.

Legislation that gives authority for specification management to Procurement should provide the ability to develop, revise, and take necessary action to achieve maximum competition by avoiding restrictive specifications, unless it is deemed to be in the best interest of the jurisdiction to purchase by emergency or sole source methods enumerated in specific conditions. This establishes the basis for procurement's responsibility to determine the method of source selection.

When procurement has authority for specification management, there is greater opportunity to achieve value. Specification management includes maintaining a library of reference materials. Generally, governments purchase the same commodities and equipment repetitively. Resources such as the Internet provide a tool to update specifications from previous purchases and look for possible alternates. Once the research is complete, the buyer and user can work together to develop a specification based upon the user's requirements and determine the method of purchase that will result in the greatest value.

The Importance of Specifications

Specifications have been described as the basic core of a purchase. They are a mechanism to tell a supplier what is needed. They should be clear, as human nature dictates interpretation of specifications just as it interprets all other information, based upon experiences. The way specifications are written impacts response and price. Poorly developed specifications are confusing and often cause problems in the bidding process, including waste, embarrassment, and protests. If specifications are vague, a supplier is not going to provide what the government has requested. If they are restrictive, there are limited responses that typically result in higher pricing. Poor specifications require clarification and addenda that generally add time to the procurement. They contradict the recognized goals of procurement—efficiency because of confusion and delays, effectiveness because the correct quality level is not achieved, and economy due to value are not being realized.

The importance of specifications cannot be overemphasized. They provide equity and competition to public sector procurement and discourage collusion. Specifications are a control mechanism to ensure quality by prohibiting unnecessary tolerances or features. They assure a level that "will do the job" instead of a preference where the level is above what is actually needed. Purchases based on well developed and appropriate specifications result in value. Finally, specifications set the stage for the evaluation process, where the response is evaluated against the criteria of the specifications for conformity and responsiveness.

Development of Specifications

*T*wo goals should drive the specification development process. The first is the requirements of the user. The focus should be on getting what the user needs, based upon intended use and the approved budget allocation. The discussions in Chapters 4 and 5 strongly support the criticality for procurement's involvement in the budget process instead of waiting until time to purchase. Procurement participation gives them an understanding of project and impact and provides an opportunity to research alternatives and determine necessary lead time.

The second goal is a results value purchase that is measured by maximum dollar value, timeliness, and integrity throughout the process. The maximum dollar value represents the savings to the jurisdiction, which may not always be the lowest price. Timeliness is an indication that delivery occurred by the needed date. The integrity of the process is judged by openness, fairness, absence of favoritism, and an equal chance to compete.

Specification Sources

An experienced buyer has strong research capabilities. This is a valuable and critical attribute for writing and is extremely important when broadening a specification to encourage competition. Today's procurement official has the advantage of the Internet in addition to resources available from various purchasing organizations, trade magazines, suppliers, and product information to produce and write a good specification.

People are another valuable source for specifications. User departments are generally the initiators of specifications. Their information forms the foundation for the buyer to build upon, even if the original specifications are restrictive. Suppliers provide information on alternative or equal products and are an excellent source to determine if the specifications are restrictive. Public procurement officials are always willing to share specifications and bid and proposal information with their colleagues.

Researching specification sources is a critical step in the process that can optimize value. As noted in the previous chapter, a single bid response due to restrictive specifications often results in delivery delays because of having to re-solicit bids. If a single bid is awarded, there is a risk of overpayment due to lack of competition. The procurement official who takes time on the front end of the process prevents problems that can be embarrassing, at the very least, and hurt credibility, at the worst. A list of potential sources for specifications is located in Appendix C.

Specification Content

A specification is defined as "a set of requirements to be satisfied by a product, material or a process showing, whenever appropriate, the procedure that will determine whether the requirements given are satisfied" (NIGP, 1996, p. 4). The term describes the product in terms of technical and descriptive requirements and may be used interchangeably with purchase description, statement of work, purchase requirement, or other similar terms. Before development of the specification, a requirements analysis process should take place where the buyer applies value analysis to specifications that will eliminate products or services that are not cost effective.

At the very least, specifications should:

- identify minimum requirements;
- allow for competition;
- describe testing methods, if applicable;
- result in an equitable award to the lowest responsive bidder;
- be simple, concise, and avoid loopholes that would allow the bidder to offer a product below the stated quality level;
- be common to at least two manufacturers; and
- identify measurable physical, functional and quality characteristics that meet the requirements, including basic design, physical dimensions, weights, percentages and types of ingredients, and types and grades of materials.

In some cases, specifications should identify a brand available in the market, have reasonable tolerances, and be flexible to allow for better products and possible cost saving alternatives.

The National Institute of Governmental Purchasing's, *General Public Procurement* (1999) describes the format that should be used for the basic content of specifications. The format should be uniform with similar requirements, and information should be included in subsections under the applicable section. The standard sections are scope, applicable publications and terminology, requirements, testing, preparation for delivery, and notes or comments. Titles of sections should be capitalized. Procurement procedures should include a standardized format for specifications in solicitation documents. Specifications should be separate from the bidder/proposer instructions, which are universal to all of an entity's bids or proposals, general conditions, and special conditions that are specific to the particular solicitation. An example of a specification format is included in Appendix D.

Types of Specifications

*T*he type of specification that should be used for any procurement depends upon the desired outcome. Those who have responsibility for preparing specifications should determine what they want to accomplish, then select the appropriate specification type. The experienced procurement official, like an experienced carpenter, selects the appropriate specification to obtain the greatest value, just as the experienced carpenter selects the correct tool to build a table.

Using the wrong specification type results in wasted time, resources and, per-haps, undesirable outcomes. Because the public sector uses a variety of com-modities and services ranging from office supplies, computer hardware and software, road materials, and chemicals to landscaping, janitorial, consultant/ design, and health services, public sector procurement officials should have expertise in all specification types and their appropriate usage. Selection of the best type of specification results in the greatest value for the government.

Specifications are often categorized as standard or custom. Standard specifi-cations are detailed, generally are used for repetitive purchases, and can be obtained quickly and easily. These are often classified as "off-the-shelf," "ready-made," or "commercially available" as compared to the custom specifications that are typically limited to a one-time procurement.

Design Specifications

Categorized as the most traditional type, a design specification enumerates how the item to be purchased is constructed or manufactured. It is used in public sector contracting for construction of and improvements to buildings, highways, and bridges that are often categorized as public works projects. Design specifications are detailed and specify exact dimensions, materials, and tolerances specific to the user's requirements. They often include engineering drawings or blueprints.

There are advantages and disadvantages to design specifications. Advantages include the user getting exactly what is specified. Evaluation is objective, based on whether the bidder is responsive to specifications. Safety requirements and standards often provide the best justification for design specifications, particularly in construction projects.

Design specifications are detailed...to the user's requirements.

The most obvious disadvantage for using design specifications is limited competition. By their very nature and requirement for preciseness, design specifications are restrictive. The objective of a design specification is to meet a custom or unique requirement. Design specifications are traditional and should not be used for purchases where the intent is to examine the latest technology or allow for innovation and cost savings.

Purchasers who desire to acquire a particular product with ease by using a supplier's catalog description in order to simplify and expedite the process may apply a design specification when buying commercial products. The result is a restrictive specification and limited competition. Using "minimum" and "maximum" for tolerances allow some latitude and flexibility but do not totally avoid limitations to only a few products.

The competitive bid method of procurement is generally used with design specifications. Award is based upon compliance with specifications to the lowest responsive and responsible bidder. This is generally considered to result in an objective process; however, problems occur when a bidder submits an alternate that meets the majority of specifications except those that are so restrictive that only one or two products or equipment comply. When the alternate can achieve significant savings and the restrictive specifications do not have a negative impact on performance, the purchaser should have the ability to deem a technicality in order to make an award in the best interest of the government.

Another common problem that purchasers face is determining compliance. It is incumbent upon the bidder, and not the buyer, to prove that a product or equipment meets specifications. While this sounds relatively simple, the process of determining equivalency can be lengthy and adversarial and lends itself to protests from the supplier.

Performance Specifications

Performance specifications focus on the result. Instead of detailing dimensions, composition, and materials, they state what is to be achieved. Where a design specification lists physical, chemical, or quality characteristics, a performance specification generally describes a product by its capacity, function, or operation (Burt & Pinkerton, 1996). Performance is the desired outcome where the supplier or proposer is given the opportunity to provide innovative methods or products that generally result in value. The words "function" and "performance" are often used interchangeably.

Instead of meeting specific dimensions or composition, performance is evaluated by tests or criteria established in the solicitation. "How to accomplish" and "what is expected" are the focus instead of compliance with details. This may be described as measurable output, performance under conditions or at intervals, or overall results. Achievement of the particular requirements is based upon ingenuity and expertise.

Performance specifications do not eliminate essential restrictions or complexity. Descriptions in the solicitation document may be detailed and lengthy to establish the foundation for the desired result. Identified as a statement of work, scope of project, or in the case of a product or equipment, required performance, the purchaser establishes minimums and details parameters that set the stage for what is to be accomplished. The bidder or proposer then has the latitude to work within this framework to provide the greatest value to meet the goals of procurement—efficiency, effectiveness and economy, and achieve the best value.

Using performance specifications provides the ability to enhance competition by encouraging creativity and alternatives. They allow the buyer to take advantage of the latest products and equipment and are widely used to procure technology. Performance specifications provide a convenient way to procure various services that can range from landscaping and janitorial to health care and professional expertise.

One disadvantage of performance specifications is subjectivity, particularly if the competitive proposal method of procurement is used. Unlike the objective bid where award is based on the lowest price meeting specifications, award of a proposal is based upon how well the offeror meets the desired results and how cost effective the solution. The proposal is graded on criteria stated in the solicitation, usually receiving a number up to the value assigned to the specific criteria. An example of criteria and assigned numerical points follows:

Experience of firm with similar projects:	35 pts.
References:	30 pts.
Approach to project:	20 pts.
Cost:	15 pts.
Total:	100 pts.

Subjectivity plays a major role when individuals score proposals, for each participant has a different perception, experience, bias, agenda, and expectation that surface in the evaluation process. In addition, the process lends itself to manipulation either by the proposer, who may know and emphasize the areas in which the user has the most interest, or the user, who purposely manipulates the scoring in order to award a favorite company.

Combination Performance and Design Specifications

Combining the performance and design types of specifications provides the ability to specify essential features, characteristics, or requirements while allowing the supplier creativity that results in cost-saving alternatives and value. The technique is widely used by public and private sector procurement professionals. Utilizing the two requires skill and expertise to determine what is truly an essential design need within the framework of performance. Care should be taken to avoid unnecessary restrictive requirements that can defeat the intent of the performance specification.

Brand Name or Approved Equivalent Specifications

The most common type of specification submitted by users is the brand name that includes the manufacturer, model, or catalog number to identify what is needed. The procurement official is challenged to determine whether the specified item is justified based upon standardization for savings, safety, or repair or is merely a request for a preferred product. A common argument of the user is that the product is the best, based upon experience. Many procurement offices require justification from the user to document the need for a specific product or equipment to avoid the perception of preference.

A brand name specification establishes a minimum level of acceptability. Items that equal or exceed this level are understood to be acceptable. Procurement officials usually add the phrase "or approved equivalent" to encourage competition. The words "or equivalent" and "or equal" should not be used without the word "approved," as it holds the purchaser responsible for equivalency instead of the supplier. The entity should have final approval authority, as it is often difficult to determine equality when features or characteristics differ among products.

While the brand name specification is the easiest to prepare and the least complex, it is restrictive and limits competition. Adding "or approved equivalent" opens the specification to a degree but encourages controversy and lessens objectivity when other than the specified product is offered. One solution is to allow more than one product. Whenever possible, the specification should include design or functional characteristics that are essential for intended use. The buyer should use brand designations that are recognized throughout a particular industry or specifications that are readily available so those suppliers know which of their products are comparable. Use of a phrase such as "no substitutes" should be kept to a minimum, unless there is adequate justification.

Some argue that a brand name product is competitive when it can be obtained from several sources. While this is not as restrictive as availability from an only source, the outcome limits competition. Many governments discourage use of brand name specifications and require that the procurement director make a written determination that only the designated brand will meet the requirements of the user.

While brand name specifications have a place in public sector procurement, they are not the best specification and use should be limited. Acceptable circumstances include when resources or time is limited, the dollar value is so low that a more complex specification is not warranted, a standardization program has been established, or a particular brand has been justified for compatibility or repair. It is best to include a statement such as:

> Any manufacturers' names, trade names, brand names or catalog numbers used in the specifications are for the purpose of describing and establishing general performance and quality levels. Such references are not intended to be restrictive. Bids are invited on these and comparable brands or products provided the quality of the proposed products meet or exceed the quality of the specification listed for any item. (NIGP, 1999, p. 6)

Samples

The use of samples as a replacement for description specifications should be minimal. A better use is a submittal of samples to supplement the specification. Uniform colors, patches or emblems, janitorial products or other commodities that require visual inspection or testing prior to award are examples where samples can help to ensure best value. Award is based on performance, or in the case of a color, how it matches with what is currently used and how well it meets the specification. A sample may be required prior to award as a prototype to determine if the final product meets the initial description or performs as needed.

Qualified Products Lists (QPL)

A qualified products list is both a tool and a type of specification. As a tool, it expedites the bidding process and simplifies award. Products are tested and evaluated prior to bidding, and suppliers are only allowed to bid on what has been approved as a qualified product. Award is made to the lowest price, or lowest approved item, on the list. The process is similar to a pre-qualification in that only what meets performance criteria is permitted.

The specification becomes the approved product. The test process to assure compliance with the specification or required result takes place outside of the bid process. Jurisdictions allow testing of new products for addition to the list either throughout the year or during a specified time window. The process is advertised and suppliers are invited to participate, which ensures that the jurisdiction meets competitive requirements.

There are several advantages to qualified products lists. The primary advantage is the expedited process by not having to delay award until all products are tested. A second advantage is the simplicity of the process. Award is made to the bidder who has submitted the lowest price on one of the previously approved products. The result is that all items are responsive and comply with the specifications.

A disadvantage occurs if procurement staff fails to keep the list current, which can cause confusion among suppliers and affect the quality level. Product specifications change, as do catalog or model numbers. Another disadvantage is that a new product cannot be bid if the supplier fails to meet the deadline for testing or if the product is introduced outside of the test window. The new product may be more cost effective but cannot be utilized until it is tested and new bids are solicited.

Good candidates for qualified products lists are those that often require testing to assure performance level. They represent wide varieties that are common and easily purchased in the marketplace. Typically, there are several responses that have the potential of delaying an award because of unfamiliarity with the product and the time required for testing. Examples include janitorial, chemical, automotive parts, batteries, and paint.

Material-and-Method Manufacture Specifications

This type of specification is used primarily by the armed forces and the Department of Energy. Potential suppliers are told precisely what materials to use and how they are to be processed. The buying organization assumes full responsibility for the performance of the products acquired under this arrangement. Large buyers of paint would use these specifications to request manufacturers to add or delete certain chemicals when producing paint for them. In the industrial sector, for reasons of health or safety, some firms dealing with chemical or pharmaceutical products also use these specifications to describe their requirements.

As in the case of design specifications, many organizations do not use material and method of manufacture specifications because of the high risks assumed by the purchaser, the relatively high costs associated with developing the specifications and inspecting the materials, and the probability of losing out on the latest advancements in technology and in manufacturing.

Adequate competition is possible, and good pricing can normally be obtained when using material-and-method manufacture specifications.

Engineering Drawings

Descriptions by blueprints or drawings are recommended when precise shapes, dimensions, close tolerances, and a high degree of manufacturing perfection are needed. Drawings may be used alone; although, normally, they accompany other purchase descriptions. Machined parts, forging, castings, construction, and special mechanical parts and components are the types of requirements that would normally justify the use of drawings.

This is an expensive method of describing requirements, both from the point of view of preparing the information and from using it in the manufacturing process. The availability of the information in an electronic format and the capability of manufacturing systems to utilize the data should help reduce some of the costs while increasing the effectiveness of this method of describing and communicating requirements.

Market Grades

Market grades are used when procuring commodities that are traded regularly on the commodity exchanges. This type of specification is generally limited to the natural products, such as lumber, cotton, tobacco, food products, wheat, hides, etc. Grading determines the quality of the commodities. It is accomplished by comparing a commodity with standards already agreed upon. Trade associations, commodity exchanges, and government agencies are very active in the development and revisions of market grades.

It should be pointed out that this method of describing materials is somewhat subjective, because the grading depends to a great extent on decisions made by inspectors. General market supply is another factor affecting quality and grading. The parameters are, therefore, broader than those found in other types of specifications. Purchasers often have to depend on the suppliers to provide the grade that was ordered. Because price is determined by the grade, it is advisable to deal with reputable firms and to obtain the services of an impartial inspector, if the total value of the order warrants such expenditures.

Standards and the Standardization Process

*T*he use of standards in the specification process is driven by the need for a consistent level. A standard focuses on quantity, value, quality, or some other type of rank or achievement that can be measured. Examples include industry standards, commercial standards, federal standards, and international standards. These standards have been evaluated and approved by an authority or agreed upon by a group where the expectation is that they will perform at the designated grade. They are recognized by classifications, test methods, or similar categories that are universally accepted and identified for components, specific parts, an entire unit, or final product.

A standard is an important tool to the procurement profession. It is easily communicated as part of specifications and understood by all parties who participate in the bid process. Good suppliers are familiar with products that have been approved by a professional society, such as the American Standards Association or the American Society for Testing and Materials, Underwriters Laboratories or trade groups, such as the National Electric Manufacturer's Association or the American Society of Mechanical Engineers. They may also include approved manufacturers.

The standardization process establishes agreement on the characteristics and quality of what is purchased. The process examines several products and then determines the desired level that will result in the greatest value for the government. The final result of a standardization process is a standard specification to be used for current and future purchases.

Standards may be established by an internal group within the organization. A standards committee is a key ingredient in the procurement process for determining the purchase. Committee members are usually comprised of representatives from user departments and procurement staff. A standards committee is normally responsible for the following:

- issuing and maintaining all standard specifications for supplies, services, and construction needed by the organization;
- revising all standard specifications;
- establishing guidelines for drafting these specifications;
- establishing standards for materials and products; and
- evaluating the products for the Qualified Products Lists.

Because a standard may limit competition and, at times, result in a non-competitive purchase, care should be taken to ensure that the standards are reasonable and that their use provides value to the organization. It is critical that the standards committee understands the public sector procurement process to assure that any restrictive specification is based on a universal standard or proven value to the government and taxpayer rather than preference for a particular product. Other committee responsibilities include revisions of standards to keep current with the market, evaluating products for qualified products lists, and reviewing user requests based on the predetermined standards. The standardization process is a team effort that requires several players with different agendas and backgrounds to work together to make decisions for the organization.

Standardization of specification provides value...

Standardization of specifications provides value in several ways. In addition to assessing requirements and setting a quality level, standardization reduces the number of items carried in inventory. This reduction encourages purchases in larger quantities that result in lower unit prices. There are also reductions in the number of items warehoused. This discourages obsolescence due to spoilage or non-use and results in reduced inventory carrying costs.

Standardization Program

*S*tandardization is the process of establishing agreement on the characteristics and quality, design, and performance of the products and services to be purchased. Standardization is a tool intended to achieve savings. The term "simplification" is often used in discussions relating to standardization. In fact, these terms have a different meaning. Standardization is essentially a technical and engineering concept, meaning agreement on designs, sizes, shapes, colors, quality, materials composition, chemical properties, performance characteristics, etc. Simplification means a reduction in the number of designs, shapes, sizes, and colors.

There are several cost-reduction features associated with a good standardization program.

- Purchasing of fewer items in larger quantities and at a lower cost is made easier.
- Purchasing is simplified, and time needed to complete transactions is shorter.
- Processing and stocking of fewer items is possible.
- Control of inventories is simplified and less costly.
- Overall operating costs can be reduced more quickly while retaining a high efficiency level.

American industry is increasing its use of standardization, mainly as a result of the rapidly expanding need to serve clients around the world. Moreover, it is in the best interests of manufacturers to adopt standards when new products are developed because of competition. The relatively high cost of standardizing after the fact is another reason for using this approach.

The need for international standards is becoming more important, and specialists in government purchasing should be aware of the developments in this regard. Generally, progress in the implementation of international standards is slow but inevitable. The American National Standards Institute (ANSI) looks after the interests of the United States in the development of international standards. The International Organization for Standardization (ISO), the International Electrotechnical Commission (IEC), the Pan American Standards commission (COPANT), ANSI, the Underwriters Laboratories (UL), the Canadian Standards Association (CSA), and the Canadian General Standards Board (CGSB) are the most important of the international voluntary standards organizations. One of the important international standards is the metric system of measurement. There are major obstacles involved in converting to the metric system in the United States, and it is unlikely that everything will ever become metric. However, there are indications that the country is slowly adopting the metric system; although, at this time (1998), products made to metric measurements account for only 6% of U.S. sales. Products made to U.S. measurements but labeled with metric equivalents will be common in the near future.

Specification Writing and Techniques

A lthough the following has been discussed earlier in the chapter, it is worth repeating in this section. Specification writing requires following a format and style that makes it clear and easily understood by the reader. A specification should accomplish four objectives:

- Identify minimum requirements.
- Allow for a competitive bid.
- List reproducible test methods for compliance assurance.
- Allow for award that is equitable.

These four objectives are critical for a purchase to result in value.

Specifications should not include any requirements that are in the General Conditions, Special Conditions, or Instructions to Bidders. Specifications are a description and should communicate what is to be purchased. Required delivery date, delivery location, payment terms, and other non-descriptive elements should be placed in other sections of the bid or proposal document.

Terms that may be unfamiliar to a bidder or proposer should be defined to avoid confusion in interpretation. These may be included in a separate section under "Definitions" or incorporated into the body of the specifications.

The following is based upon the National Institute of Governmental Purchasing's *Specifications* (2000) text and is a generally accepted guide for a specification format.

Measurements

Dimensions, gauges, capacities, size designations, volume, or temperatures should be specified in accordance with established precedent and trade practice for the particular commodity or service to be purchased. Whenever possible, words should be replaced with numbers; tolerances should be specified, where applicable; and the use of "minimum" and "maximum" should be used, wherever practicable.

Figures and Tables

Writers should use figures, illustrations, tables, and graphs whenever possible to clarify descriptions and demonstrate relationships.

Type, Class, Grade, Composition and Other Classifications

Use of these classifications should be in accordance with established precedence and trade practices for the type of equipment, materials, or supplies being purchased. *Type* applies to differences in design, model, shape, and other similar characteristics of the items. *Class* implies differences in mechanical or other characteristics of items that do not constitute a difference in quality or grade. *Grade* represents differences in quality of a commodity. When practicable, the first grade of a commodity should be the highest or best grade. *Composition* is used to classify commodities that are differentiated strictly by their respective chemical compositions. *Other classifications,* such as form, weight, size, power, supply, temperature rating, condition, insulation, etc., suitable for reference for the applicable equipment or commodity item may be used.

Sampling, Inspection, and Testing

These tools assure that the items offered are responsive by meeting the specifications. While they are not necessary for all purchases, the skilled procurement professional and the user department should not hesitate to utilize them to assure compliance.

Preparation for Delivery

Specifications should always describe how the items are to be packaged, packed, and marked. Any special conditions should be noted in the document.

Specification Writing Style

The degree to which specifications are open or restrictive directly affects the type and extent of the competition obtained. In addition, specifications provide a control to ensure that a proper quality level is purchased and that the item is suited for the intended use without unnecessary features that increase costs. Specifications are public records that ensure the integrity of the process with their openness by allowing the public access to what is being purchased. They serve as a benchmark in the evaluation process.

For these reasons, specifications should be written carefully. A skilled specification writer wants the audience to understand what is needed. A procurement official's audience is diverse, ranging from differences in language and culture, level of education and experience, and training in the particular industry. Language should be clear, concise, simple, and easy to follow, preferably using the active instead of passive voice. Words and phrases should be direct and to the point. By identifying the essential characteristics of the items to be purchased, potential suppliers know what is requested so that they can accurately compute their bids.

Writers should be cognizant of words and phrases and how they impact a bidder's understanding and, consequently, what is offered. Use of mandatory words, such as "shall" and "will," express a binding requirement that if not followed, results in a non-responsive bid. Often, user departments will copy manufacturer's product sheets to use as specifications that include mandatory language. Procurement officials should be aware of this, as failure to open language, where applicable, results in restricted specifications and limited competition.

On the other side, procurement officials should be aware of problems associated with the words "may" and "should" that express non-mandatory provisions. If these are used where a more stringent requirement should apply, the result is a sub-standard specification and quality level that does not meet the needs of the user.

Pre-bid and Pre-proposal Conferences

Pre-bid and pre-proposal conferences are becoming a standard element in the bid and the proposal processes. They are a mechanism to clarify the documents and eliminate misunderstandings and misinterpretations. Everyone who attends has an opportunity to ask questions, and the same information is presented at one time. Those who are unable to attend are notified by addendum of changes and clarifications. Addenda should be mailed to all potential suppliers or contractors who were originally mailed a solicitation document.

Conclusion

Specification development follows requirements determination and builds upon it. Omitting the planning step significantly impacts the intent of the solicitation. The result is little or no value because of failure to research and analyze history and alternatives that may realize significant savings.

Because of pressure from their users to get an item quickly, procurement officials generally do not have adequate time to do research. This causes the specification development process to be fragmented, often restrictive and poorly constructed. Frequently, the solicitation is a duplicate of a previous purchase without regard to alternate products, new suppliers, and usage and performance history. This enforces the need for procurement to be an active participant in the planning process in order to know what will be requested during the year so that schedules can be implemented for anticipated lead time.

Specification writing should be a dual activity between the user and procurement office. A buyer should understand what the users need and work with them to accomplish this. At the same time, a buyer has responsibility to select the proper specification type and determine the appropriate method of procurement. If greater value can be achieved by a competitive method, then a buyer should search for qualified sources. If a single source is the best solution, a buyer should be competent in justifying the purchase.

Because specifications are the lifeblood and basic core of the purchase, procurement officials should have excellent writing and development skills. Possible problem areas include the diversity of the audience and the potential of bidders to interpret specifications based upon their own experiences. Writers should avoid gray areas by defining terms and referencing standards as a benchmark.

Specifications set the stage for the evaluation process. Poorly written specifications cause confusion that results in incorrect products being offered. Omissions form the basis for change orders and additional costs during the contract administration period. Procurement is charged with recognizing and correcting weak specifications in the development stage to avoid problems in the implementation stage.

Finally, specifications should be open to ensure the integrity of the procurement process. Suppliers who provide initial assistance to users in specification development should understand that the process is competitive and impartial to all qualified offerors who can furnish the product or service.

References

American Bar Association (2000). *The 2000 Model Procurement Code for State and Local Governments.* Washington, DC: American Bar Association.

Burt, D. N., Ph.D., & Pinkerton, R. L., Ph.D., C.P.M. (1996). *A purchasing manager's guide to strategic proactive procurement* (Chapter 3). New York: American Management Association.

Hough, H. E., & Ashley, J. M. (1992). *Handbook of buying and purchasing management* (Chapters 4 and 5). Englewood Cliffs, NJ: Prentice Hall.

Kelman, S. (1990). *Procurement and public management* (Chapters 3 and 4). Washington, DC: The AEI Press.

National Association of State Procurement Officials (NASPO) (2001). *State & local government purchasing principles & practices* (Chapter 5). Lexington, KY: NASPO.

National Institute of Governmental Purchasing, Inc. (NIGP) (1996). *Dictionary of purchasing terms* (5th ed.). Herndon, VA: NIGP.

National Institute of Governmental Purchasing, Inc. (NIGP) (1999). *General public procurement.* Herndon, VA: NIGP.

National Institute of Governmental Purchasing, Inc. (NIGP) (2000). *Specifications.* Herndon, VA: NIGP

CHAPTER 7

Pricing Strategies

*T*he final stage of planning, scheduling, and requirements analysis includes selection of the best pricing strategy. The skilled procurement official should have sufficient knowledge and expertise to select a pricing method that results in the greatest value to the government. Previous chapters addressed quality as an element of minimum value and maximum value. A value-results purchase is based on the required quality level being obtained at the lowest cost.

As in the case of planning, requirements, and value analysis, and specification development, the average buyer does not take sufficient time to examine requests to apply the best pricing strategy. Similar to the other phases of the procurement cycle, time is not always available to get the product or service quickly due to the pressures of user departments. The tendency is to develop bid or proposal documents resulting in award to the low responsive bidder or the highest scored offeror, depending on the legal requirements that regulate the method of source selection.

This chapter discusses evaluation techniques that procurement officials can use to maximize value to the organization. The discussion on supplier pricing strategies illustrates the link to requirements determination, particularly the planning and scheduling components. Prior to preparation of specifications and solicitation, time must be taken up front to research market conditions, price history fluctuation, assess available competition and the characteristics of the industry, and develop an understanding of the supplier marketplace to enable the buyer to make decisions that are based upon value.

Procurement professionals should realize the importance of selecting the right suppliers. This step is another critical element in the procurement cycle that takes place after determination of pricing strategy. In order to realize the best price, procurement officials must first select the best source. The skilled procurement official understands supplier-pricing strategies and utilizes this knowledge to determine a fair and reasonable price. Pricing strategy is based upon demand in the marketplace, the elements of cost without profit, and what the competition may offer. A solid understanding of this process is essential to selecting the appropriate procurement method and type of contract.

Discussions in this chapter focus on price analysis, cost analysis and life-cycle costing as evaluation techniques used to maximize value. These are critical tools in the procurement profession that are often underutilized due to time constraints and procurement being omitted from the initial budget process.

Supplier Pricing Strategies

*H*ow the supplier determines price requires an understanding of several economic principles. Price is only one element of the total cost of the product or service. The supplier first looks at supply and demand when calculating total price in terms of what the buyer is willing to pay. When there is an ample supply of the product and sufficient competition, the price is generally low. Conversely, when supply is low and there are limited suppliers, the price increases.

The market is identified as stable or unstable. The laws of supply and demand characterize stable markets. Buyers who understand the dynamics of stable markets know that products are easily obtainable as off-the-shelf. Prices may decrease, so any type of long-term contract should include the ability to de-escalate prices.

The unstable market is characterized by fluctuating prices that are influenced by outside factors. Examples include raw materials that are subject to unpredictable conditions, such as weather, financial upheavals, or political instability. Unstable markets are typically not subject to supply and demand, and there are often more buyers wanting to purchase a product or service than sellers. Scheduling becomes an important element, if the desired purchase result is value.

Competition

Competition is the availability of more than one supplier who is willing to provide the requested product or service. A market where there is perfect competition follows supply and demand, characterized by a sufficient number of suppliers who are able to compete. In this environment, buyers only need minimal knowledge about the market to obtain value, since there are adequate numbers of sellers willing to participate in the process.

An oligopoly occurs when there are a limited number of sellers. Another type of limited competition is a monopoly, where there is only one seller. In these situations, buyers must be more familiar with the market to purchase effectively. This is particularly true for a monopoly market where only one company can provide the needed product or service. Since there are generally many buyers, the seller is able to dictate price and conditions. In this scenario, the buyer must understand the market, continually search for alternatives, and have excellent negotiation skills to obtain the best value.

From the seller's point of view, a fair and reasonable price is one that is based upon the direct costs that include raw materials and labor, indirect costs, and a reasonable profit. Indirect costs are often identified as overhead or general sale and administrative costs. These include additional expenses associated with basic labor costs, such as vacation, sick leave, insurance and taxes, and utility costs (NIGP, Advanced Public Procurement, 2000).

The buyer views a fair and reasonable price based upon the level of need for the item. What the buyer is willing to pay depends on urgency, availability in the marketplace, and whether alternatives are available.

The skilled procurement professional understands the difference between price, cost and profit. According to the National Institute of Governmental Purchasing's *Dictionary of Purchasing Terms,* price includes "all costs (direct labor, overhead, materials) and profit or fee." Cost represents "the actual expenses incurred in delivering a product, service or construction. It includes both direct and indirect costs but does not include fee or profit for the supplier." Profit is defined as "the difference between the costs incurred by the supplier to provide the supplies, services and the amount received from the purchaser in payment" (NIGP, 1996, pp. 22, 62, 65).

A more succinct definition is offered by Burt and Pinkerton (1996) in *A Purchasing Manager's Guide to Strategic Proactive Procurement.* Cost is all elements of expense with the exception of profit. Price includes all elements of expense plus profit. Profit is determined from the net proceeds obtained by deducting all elements of cost from the price. Expressed as a simple equation, *Cost + Profit = Price*.

Seller Pricing Strategies

*T*he National Institute of Governmental Purchasing's *Advanced Public Procurement* (1999) identifies four pricing strategies that are representative of public procurement theory. The first, *cost-based pricing* occurs when a margin of profit is added to reasonable labor, material, and overhead costs. The second, *market-based pricing*, takes place when pricing is contingent on the customer's current demand and a willingness of the competitors to supply similar products or services. *Value-based pricing* is based upon the perceived or actual value that the buyer will receive. The final strategy is the *market-oriented pricing* model, where prices are defined according to the range of the quality of the product or service provided by the supplier (Burt & Pinkerton, 2000).

Pricing strategy is based upon a particular industry. The supplier generally uses a cost-based pricing strategy for the more standardized products and services and a market-oriented strategy for those products and services that are non-standard or specialized (NIGP, 1998, p. 62). Because most suppliers provide more than one item, some of the products may be cost based and some market based. This affects profit margin, as the seller generally sells different products at different margin levels to achieve an overall satisfactory profit. This is important to buyers when purchasing in different market types and at different levels of competition.

According to Burt and Pinkerton (1996), procurement can realize good pricing by following several prerequisites, including the right amount of competition; adequate price analysis; thorough cost analysis when price analysis is inadequate or inappropriate; selecting the right method of contract pricing and the right contract; partnerships and long-term contracts; and use of negotiation rather than competitive bidding where appropriate. They also advocate applying the principles of Zero Base Pricing similar to Zero Base Budgeting.

There are two additional pricing strategies that buyers should be aware of that can dramatically affect procurement value. Loss leader, commonly known as "low balling," occurs when a seller offers a price that is significantly lower than other bids. The bidder may be an unknown who is willing to provide the product or service in anticipation of future business where pricing would be higher, or the bidder may lack sufficient experience to perform and has incorrectly calculated the necessary materials or other costs required for the job. If this bidder receives the award, the jurisdiction may be the victim of high price change orders or poor workmanship. It is procurement's responsibility to the user to thoroughly research the bidder to determine responsiveness and responsibility.

Offset pricing occurs when a bidder offers a low price for the basic services. Higher profit requirements cost significantly more. Buyers who are responsible for construction contracts should be particularly careful to ensure that change orders are negotiated at reasonable prices.

Supplier Selection

*U*nderstanding market conditions and the availability of competition are critical steps in the supplier selection process. A buyer should have knowledge of the supplier base, if the commodity or service is one that is frequently purchased. When there is unfamiliarity with a request, the buyer should take time to research the market in order to select the best suppliers.

Governments typically have a bidder's list that houses the names of vendors and contractors who request bids and proposals. A large government often has an extensive list. A problem that occurs when mailing to all potential bidders listed in a commodity or service category on a bidder's list is the possibility of selecting vendors who cannot meet the requirements. Even with a bidder's list, buyers should take time to ensure that those selected to receive solicitations can actually provide the product or service. While some jurisdictions require that solicitations be mailed to all on the list, either electronically or by regular mail, the procurement profession is moving towards an e-Procurement process where solicitations are posted on a Web site. Potential bidders can either download or request documents via telephone or e-mail. This method targets the supplier who has the capability to meet the solicitation requirements and broadens the competition base. At the same time, it increases the number of unfamiliar suppliers, which requires a thorough evaluation in the award process.

Selecting the wrong suppliers typically results in responses with high prices, no bids, or only one bid. Buyers who overcompensate by mailing solicitations to all suppliers on a bidder's list in an attempt to avoid confrontation due to purpose or mistaken omission cause increased administrative time and mailing costs. While the public sector does not permit exclusion of potential suppliers without sufficient justification—and the general rule is that those who request solicitations receive them—the initial invitation list generally does not require mailing to all suppliers on the bidder's list.

Like other steps in the procurement process, successful supplier selection is based upon thorough research and evaluation that includes current and past performance, knowledge of the industry, and the degree of competition. The selection of the right source is the primary determining factor for the right price. Closely linked to the requirements determination process, source selection should be based on evaluating past performance on familiar suppliers, analyzing market conditions and available competition and researching capabilities, and reputations of potential suppliers. Commonly known as "strategic sourcing," it provides the foundation for successful buyer/supplier relationships results in value procurement.

Evaluation Strategies

Another step in the procurement process is evaluation. It is an important element in the cycle that enables buyers and users to determine value. Evaluation is based upon examination of price and cost, which have previously been identified as components of supplier pricing strategy. In this section, they are discussed as evaluation techniques for the buyer to assure a fair and reasonable price.

Price Analysis

Price analysis is defined as "the process of examining and evaluating price data without evaluating the separate cost elements or proposed profit" (NIGP, 1996, p. 22). The process involves comparing prices with previous purchases, similar commodities or services, or estimates prepared by an engineer, contractor, or other party. It is based on comparison without breaking down components that make up the price.

The price analysis technique is valid only if there is adequate competition resulting in a fair and reasonable price. Simply comparing the current price to the previous price paid is not necessarily valid. Even if the price is lower than what was previously paid, the buyer should canvas the market to ensure that the product is in line with current conditions.

Procurement professionals should not be misled by general procurement guidelines. Higher quantities do not necessarily result in lower prices, and several bid responses do not necessarily indicate adequate competition. For example, distributors may submit courtesy bids for their manufacturers that are higher than normal pricing. The buyer who does not compare bids to catalogs or market price typically pays more than if the price were negotiated with the manufacturer or sole supplier.

Price analysis is used extensively with the competitive sealed bid method of procurement. Contracts are based upon price, ranging from firm fixed price to fixed price with economic adjustments or fixed price with re-determination. The seller assumes risk, as price cannot change except by the terms of the contract.

Several conditions should be present in order to assure a fair and reasonable price: two or more qualified bidders have responded to the solicitation; the bids are responsive to the requirements; the suppliers competed independently for the award; the supplier submitting the lowest offer does not have an unfair advantage over the competition; and the lowest evaluated price is reasonable (NIGP, 1998, p. 4).

Competition is

Burt and Pinkerton (1996) have identified several mechanisms that can be utilized for analysis to determine a fair and reasonable price. Competition is preferred, followed by catalog or market analysis, price comparisons, engineer estimates, and negotiation.

preferred

The buyer should take necessary steps to determine if adequate competition is available to compare offers based on historical information, market price, catalog price and prices set by laws or regulations, and judgment.

Cost Analysis

Price analysis is a comparative technique. Cost analysis is an evaluation of actual and anticipated components that comprise price. The result of both techniques should be a fair and reasonable price; however, a purchaser examines a seller's costs during the cost analysis process instead of comparing it to other prices.

The NIGP's *Dictionary of Purchasing Terms* (1996) defines cost analysis as "the review and evaluation of cost data for the purpose of arriving at costs actually incurred, prices to be paid and costs to be reimbursed." The cost review is based upon categories that include direct costs, comprised of labor and materials, and indirect costs that include overhead costs and general administrative expenses. The final component is profit. Material and labor costs are straightforward and easily verified as direct costs allocated to the project. More difficult to analyze is indirect cost that refers to the additional expenses associated with personnel such as vacation, sick leave, and insurance. General and administrative expenses are other overhead costs that include rent, utilities, building insurance, and maintenance.

Cost analysis is generally associated with the competitive sealed proposal method of procurement. Proposers should submit all costs associated with the project. These are negotiated between the purchaser and the seller to determine if they can be allocated. The purchaser should also determine if costs are allowable under the terms of the contract.

The result of cost analysis is a cost-based contract that is based upon reimbursement, where the contractor is reimbursed for all allowable costs incurred plus an agreed-upon fee. Procurement officials should be aware that the purchaser assumes the risk in cost-type contracts. Of particular concern to the public sector is the cost plus a percentage of the cost-type contract where the contractor is reimbursed for all costs plus a specified percentage on top of the costs. Any type of cost contract should include an incentive to minimize costs.

Life-Cycle Costing

Life-cycle costing is a technique that determines the total cost of ownership of an asset from purchase to disposal. It involves greater analysis than basing a purchase solely on the acquisition price. Life-cycle costing also includes operating, maintenance, and disposal costs. The result may initially be a higher acquisition price but a lower price over the life of the equipment because of greater productivity and lower operating costs.

Life-cycle costing is identified as the total cost of ownership that includes the acquisition cost, installation and startup, operating costs, such as fuel, training, salaries, maintenance, insurance, and salvage, including possible trade-in.

The total cost of ownership analysis can be applied to technology purchases. The total cost would include an acquisition price that includes shipping and installation, future upgrades, license and maintenance fees, training, supplies and utility and insurance.

Because life-cycle costing is a mechanism to evaluate and a basis for award, the conditions should be stated in the solicitation document. Bidders should understand that award will be based on the lowest total cost of ownership rather than the initial purchase price.

Conclusion

*T*he final stage in the requirements determination process is evaluation. There are a number of techniques available to procurement officials, based on the same time constraints cited in earlier chapters. Price, cost, supplier pricing strategies, and life-cycle costing are evaluation tools that result in value.

Procurement officials should understand the basic principles of economics and market operations in order to be effective professionals. If they lack knowledge of competition and how a supplier bases his price, then they do not have the ability to achieve value.

Interestingly, there are no two procurements exactly alike; each is different in some respect, whether it is in the solicitation, response from vendors, protests, or specification changes. The procurements that appear to be simple are often the most difficult. When buyers take the easy approach and issue a solicitation exactly as the previous one without analyzing, meeting with the user, researching possible cost saving alternatives, and determining if there are pricing strategies that could be applied, the result is a problem purchase with little or no value. This is why procurement officers should encourage their staff to strive for the ideal as much as possible. One procurement idealist very aptly described it as "buyers need to set aside the time to identify opportunities, prioritize them to maximize returns, plan time to conduct an analysis and do it" (NIGP, 1999, p. 6).

References

Burt, D. N., Ph.D., & Pinkerton, R. L., Ph.D., C.P.M. (1996). *A purchasing manager's guide to strategic proactive procurement* (Chapter 3). New York: American Management Association.

Fearon, H. E., Dobler, D. W., & Killen, K. H. (1993). *The purchasing handbook* (5th ed). New York: McGraw Hill.

Hough, H. E., & Ashley, J. M. (1992). *Handbook of buying and purchasing management* (Chapters 4 and 5). Englewood Cliffs, NJ: Prentice Hall.

Leenders, M. R., & Flynn, A. E. (1995). *Value-driven purchasing: Managing the key steps in the acquisition process.* Tempe, AZ: McGraw Hill.

National Institute of Governmental Purchasing, Inc. (NIGP) (1996). *Dictionary of purchasing terms* (5th ed.). Herndon, VA: NIGP.

National Institute of Governmental Purchasing, Inc. (NIGP) (1999). *Advanced public procurement.* Herndon, VA: NIGP.

National Institute of Governmental Purchasing, Inc. (NIGP) (1999). *Intermediate public procurement.* Herndon, VA: NIGP.

CHAPTER 8

Conclusion

A strategic plan is a practical action-oriented guide, based on the examination of internal and external factors, which directs an agency and its resource allocations to produce meaningful results for the consumer of the jurisdiction's goods and services. While the primary focus of strategic planning is the thought process, a written document gives an agency the opportunity to describe the fundamental challenges it faces, what makes them critical, and their relative importance. Its goals, objectives, and strategies describe how it plans to respond to those challenges.

The strategic planning team suggests the content of the plan and how it will be compiled and written. The team itself may undertake the entire assignment; the workgroups used throughout the process may be asked to write up assigned sections; or a single person or unit may be designated to compile the information and write it up. The senior managers make the final assignment. An agency should tailor its plan to meet its needs. Some of the most frequently included elements are described below:

Mission Statement

    The agency's unique reason for existence

Overview of the Plan

Discussion of the Benefits an Agency Expects from the Process

Recognition of Agency Accomplishments

Brief Description of the Planning Process Used and its Participants

Explanation of the plan's elements and how to use them

Summary of Agency Mandates

Description of the mandates and their sources

Constituent Analysis

Description of constituents and their relative priority

Discussion of their expectations and the agency's ability to meet them

Core Business Activities

Description of the core business activities

Discussion of the priority for an agency's activities

Situation Assessment

Description of the external trends and issues likely to impact the agency

Discussion of the opportunities and threats

Agency Operations

Analysis of the internal operations of the agency

Discussion of the agency's internal strengths and weaknesses

Critical Issues

Description of the critical issues the agency faces and the challenges they present

Explanation of the issues' priority

Strategic Summary

Goals the agency desires to pursue

Objectives that describe the specific outcomes

Description of how the agency proposes to move in the preferred direction

Assignment of responsibility for the actions

Tracking and Evaluation

Process to monitor progress

Role of performance measures

Description of key performance measures

A coordinator collects the plan's elements and integrates the pieces to tell a story about the agency, where it is now, its desires and aspirations, and how it expects to achieve them. The strategic planning team reviews the draft and coordinates a review process.

When the reviews are completed, the strategic planning team produces and distributes the plan to agency staff. The finished document should be attractive, useful, and meaningful to agency staff. A professional appearance conveys its level of importance. The strategic planning team schedules orientation sessions to introduce and discuss the plan. To the extent practical, the agency head should be heavily involved in the meetings. Having the agency head pronounce his/her commitment to and support of the strategic plan is an excellent way to convey its importance. An agency improves its likelihood of a successful implementation when it adequately prepares staff for what is planned.

The strategic plan should undergo an annual assessment. This helps an agency:

- evaluate progress toward the goals and objectives;
- determine what went well and what lessons were learned;
- modify the plan to make it more realistic or challenging, depending upon the circumstances; and
- prepare useful information for the next planning cycle.

The report summarizes the findings of the assessment. It may be sent to agency staff and key constituents to update them on the plan.

While the strategic plan forms the broad framework within which an agency operates, the plan is generally implemented through a series of short-term action plans (sometimes referred to simply as action planning, operational planning, yearly planning, or tactical planning). Action planning links an agency's strategic goals and objectives to its day-to-day operations. While an agency uses a six-year planning horizon for its strategic plan, the action plan concentrates on what the agency can do within a specific year to execute its strategic direction. Therefore, action plans describe operations, procedures, and processes. They tell who does what and when it is to be done. It is also a tool to track and report on progress toward the strategic goals. The action plan guides the individual, section, or unit actions

Action planning links an agency's strategic goals and objectives to its day-to-day operations.

that move the agency in its preferred direction. The plan's specificity enables an agency to compute the resource requirements needed for every action and uses that information to prepare budget requests. Senior management decides how to proceed with action planning. The resulting action plan describes the portion of the strategic plan that an agency will implement over a specific time period, generally a year. It lists and sets the priority for the short-term or operational goals. Action planning can be subdivided into two components. The first is the responsibility of senior management and, the second, the individual program, division, section, or unit staff. Senior management decides the portion of the strategic plan that an agency will address. They share this with the agency and make assignments.

To be at its most effective, procurement should have a role in strategic planning for the organization, particularly in the budget process.

The unit that receives an assignment develops a work plan for implementing its part of the strategic plan. They describe the specific action steps and assign responsibility for completion, along with the expected time frame and needed resources. The resource needs (human, physical and financial) feed directly into the capital and operating budget requests, as well as into the human and information resource management processes. Information that identifies the steps, the responsible parties, time frame, and needed resources is compiled into an action plan. A tracking and monitoring system should be established to track progress.

An agency is reminded that the action plan is a short-term (1-2 year) plan. It helps the agency see exactly what must be accomplished each year to move in the direction outlined by the strategic plan and what inputs are required, who is responsible, and when each task should be completed. This information supports budget development and guides the annual operating plan. Staff receives a copy of the action plan. A briefing from managers should follow distribution. Successful implementation depends on all employees understanding the plan and their part in it. Management needs to be deliberate in seeing that this is accomplished.

To be most effective, procurement should have a role in strategic planning for the organization, particularly in the budget process. Without its participation, strategic planning is fragmented and without value, because procurement's role has been delegated to be reactive, responding to what has already been decided. When a user is ready to purchase, there typically is a limited window for the procurement staff to strategically plan in order to maximize value.

Strategic planning in procurement should occur in two phases. When procurement is involved in the budget process as a strategic player, staff is able to plan for the upcoming capital and operating purchases. There is opportunity to evaluate the market, research alternatives, and meet required delivery dates, particularly if there is a long lead time. This process is an internal strategic plan for the procurement function that follows and supports the initial strategic planning, or budgeting process.

Procurement should also have a strategic plan that incorporates all of the elements previously listed. An assessment of the function and its operation on an annual basis is critical to success. The process should identify strengths and weaknesses of the procurement office, needs of the organization based on resources, priorities and expectations of key leaders and players, criticality of projects and operations, and performance measures that meet organizational goals and objectives. The result should be an action plan that supports the organizational strategic plan.

APPENDIX A

Roles of Key Stakeholders in Strategic Planning

This appendix attempts to identify some of the potential roles assumed by the key stakeholders within an organization, as suggested by the City of Grande Prairie, Canada. It is by no means the definitive source of all the potential roles of stakeholders in government, nor is it intended to limit participant participation in various stages of strategic planning. Its main intent is to inform the reader about some of the possible roles that each stakeholder can assume. In situations when participants are unsure of their roles, the list can serve as a guide to team members in anticipating possible roles.

Chief Elected Official (typically, the Mayor or Manager/Governor)

- To guide the legislative body in its roles and responsibilities; and
- To unify and lead the legislative body and citizens in alignment of their combined expectations.

Legislative Body

- To act as sponsor of the strategic planning initiative by providing support and committing resources;
- To provide direction for the strategic planning process concerning current conditions and the planning process;
- To review with the Strategic Planning Committee issues presented to various local Boards and Agencies;
- To review with the Strategic Planning Committee the overall conclusions concerning current conditions;
- To establish planning parameters;
- To review and revise the organization's Mission, Vision, Values, Focus Areas, and Goals;
- To review and revise master plans for linkage to and alignment with the strategic plan;
- To review and approve service priorities without reference to available resources;
- To review and approve both a revised service package with preliminary resource allocation and the final service package; and
- To review and approve final plans and associated budgets.

Chief Executive Officer (if different than the Chief Elected Official)

- To act as champion of the planning process, setting the direction for the required changes;
- To guide the planning process as chairman of a Strategic Planning Committee;
- To guide administration in its roles and responsibilities for accomplishing the strategic plan.

Chief Procurement Officer

- To act as co-champion of the planning process by directing energy toward achieving its planning objectives and by coordinating its implementation;
- To guide and coordinate the various departments in assisting with the procurement aspects of the S.W.O.T. (strengths, weaknesses, opportunities and threats) analyses, resource allocation, budget preparation, and performance evaluation;
- To provide assistance and leadership to the Strategic Planning Committee in carrying out their responsibilities for financial analysis, review, and evaluation; and
- To develop the consolidated summary of the strategic plans.

Strategic Planning Committee (Origination Committee)

- To manage organizational systems, practices, and people to implement the plan;
- To oversee preparation of S.W.O.T. analyses;
- To oversee preparation of S.W.O.T. conclusions about current conditions and to submit conclusions to Council for review and feedback;
- To review current program performance in relation to legislative and citizen expectations;
- To review, approve, and present to the legislature the recommended service priorities without reference to available resources;
- To prepare, review, and approve a final consolidated service package for presentation to the legislative body (for its review and approval);
- To monitor and evaluate operations to maintain accountability and ensure that progress against the plan is measured and managed; and
- To review and evaluate both the completed year's operations and the planning process itself.

Service Level Planning Committee (Strategy Committee)

- To provide expertise on the techniques and process aspects of the planning process;

- To create linkages that ensure information flow, and coordinate implementation activities;

- To coordinate departmental surveys of citizen expectations (so that the same questions are not asked twice and are included for the benefit of staff departments);

- To conduct a review of current conditions, issues, etc., and present conclusions to the Strategic Planning Committee;

- To check the alignment of departmental strategic plans with the strategic plan and among departments; and

- To identify both the low-priority services, which will be left undone, and the delivery consequences of the planned service package.

Department Administrators

- To conduct surveys of citizen expectations with coordination by Strategic Planning Committee;

- To review and revise departmental Mission, Vision, Values, Focus Areas, and Goals;

- To draft departmental service levels and priorities; and

- To prepare cost figures for Council-approved service levels with Finance department.

APPENDIX B

Quantitative and Qualitative Evaluation Indicators

EFFICIENCY: Factors assessing effort and cost involved in acquiring needed goods and services.

- Quantitative
  - Administrative savings as a result of reduction in paperwork;
  - Administrative savings as a result of using blanket purchase orders;
  - Ratio of purchasing department's operating costs to dollar purchases; and
  - Ratio of purchasing employees to total employees.

- Qualitative
  - Practices followed in delegating purchasing authority to other departments;
  - Practices followed in providing financial and non-financial rewards for performance;
  - Proper selection and training of buyers; and
  - Organizational structure that encourages individual action and effective teamwork.

ECONOMY: Factors assessing savings, product, or service improvements due to purchasing actions.

- Quantitative
  - Measure of purchasing's contribution to inventory control by the extent of savings attributable to stockless purchasing;
  - Extent of cost reductions attributable to the development of new supply sources;
  - Extent of cost reductions attributable to the use of value analysis; and
  - Extent of cost reductions attributable to consolidation or standardization.

- Qualitative
  - Purchasing's awareness of in-house versus contracting-out decisions;

- Participation by purchasing personnel in outside professional activities;
- Use of price analysis to assess reasonableness of prices obtained; and
- Improvement in service or end-product due to purchasing action.

EFFECTIVENESS: Factors assessing degree that purchasing caused needed goods and services to be delivered when it was required and at an acceptable level of quality.

- **Quantitative**
  - Measure of purchasing's contribution to inventory control by the relationship between inventory levels or turnover to related requisition volume;
  - Reduction in the frequency of executing rush orders (emergency purchases);
  - Measure of purchasing's contribution to inventory control by the ratio of product rejections to the total number of completed purchase orders; and
  - Measure of purchasing's contribution to inventory control by the ratio of the number of purchase orders, where delivery was overdue when received, to the total number of completed purchase orders.

- **Qualitative**
  - Existence of a purchasing manual that clearly defines authority and responsibility;
  - Purchasing's responsibilities, including the disposition of scrap, inventory and traffic control, and invoice processing;
  - Ordering departments consult with purchasing before procurement decisions are made; and
  - Establish economic order quantities for approved inventory control.

APPENDIX C

Specification and Standards Sources

Specifications

The United States Government

American Society for Testing and Materials (ASTM)

Canadian General Standards Board

The U.S. Standards Institute

Federal, State, Provincial, Regional, County, and Local Governments

National Institute of Governmental Purchasing, Inc.

Consumer Report

Buyers Laboratory

Dataquest's Spec Check

Using Agencies

Associations of users, manufacturers, and technical societies

Colleges, universities, and technical institutes

Trade associations and independent research and testing organizations

Federal Bureau of Specifications

Standards

American National Standards Institute (ANSI)

American Society for Quality Control (ASQC)

Canadian Standards Association (CSA)

Canadian General Standards Board (CGSB)

International Organization for Standardization (ISO)

National Bureau of Standards (NBS)

National Institute of Standards and Technology (NIST)

National Lumber Manufacturers Association (NLMA)

Society for Automotive Engineers (SAE)

Society of Mechanical Engineers (SME)

APPENDIX D

Specification Format

A six-section format is the preferred format so that similar requirements and information will always appear in sub-sections under the applicable section. The sections are:

> Scope,
>
> Applicable Publications and Terminology,
>
> Requirements,
>
> Testing,
>
> Preparation for Delivery, and
>
> Notes.

Scope

This purchase description applies to wood veneer freestanding desk product components available with fixed height work surfaces and panel legs for use by government employees.

> 1.2. Executive office desk product components meeting this purchase description shall meet all the mandatory requirements of the 7th draft of AAAA.22.445 "Government Freestanding Office Desk Products and Components," as well as the mandatory options and features detailed herein. The requirements contained in this purchase description are the minimum required features and components to be accepted under this solicitation. Manufacturers may offer additional products that are designed to enhance the function of the furniture system. Acceptance of products not specified therein is at the purchaser's discretion.

Applicable Publications and Terminology

> Definitions
>
> Applicable Publications

Requirements

> General Requirements
>
> Detailed Requirements
>
> Detailed Requirements Components

Testing

Preparation for Delivery

Notes

GLOSSARY

Accountability: the method used to measure results.

Accrual Basis: a basis of accounting in which transactions are recognized at the time they are incurred, as opposed to when cash is received or spent.

Adoption: the approval of the budget by the governing body of the entity.

Allot: to divide an appropriation into amounts which may be encumbered or expended during an allotment period.

Appropriation Orders or Ordinances: constitute the legal basis for the ensuing budget period expenditures.

Audit: a methodical examination and review of records and documents, with confirmation by physical inspection or otherwise, of a situation or condition (as within a purchasing office), concluding with a detailed report of findings.

Bidder's List: a collection of names and addresses of vendors from whom bids, proposals, or quotations can be solicited.

Brainstorming: a formal process designed to engage participants in a conference designed to generate ideas.

Brand Name Specification: a specification using one or more manufacturers' brand names, with identifying model numbers, to describe the standards of quality, performance, and other characteristics needed to meet the requirements of a solicitation and which invites bids for equivalent products from any manufacturer.

Budget Message: a communication normally written by the chief executive that accompanies the budget estimate. Its purpose is to explain: (1) the main points of the budget; (2) the assumptions under which it was assembled; and (3) the major policy recommendations.

Capital Budgets: explains and identifies the outlays for major acquisitions of long-term assets.

Combination Specification: has features of both design specifications and performance specifications.

Commodity/Service Code: a system of numbers or descriptions designated to identify and list commodities or services by classes and sub-classes.

Competition: the effort of two or more vendors to secure the business of a purchaser by the offer of the most favorable terms as to price, quality, and promptness of delivery and/or service.

Cost: actual expenses incurred in delivering a product, service, or construction. Includes both direct and indirect costs but not the fee or profit for the vendor.

Cost Analysis: the review and evaluation of cost data for the purpose of arriving at costs actually incurred or estimates of costs to be incurred, prices to be paid, and costs to be reimbursed.

Customer Survey: a general examination of a situation or topic, with the intent to account for certain concepts.

Design Specification: a specification establishing the characteristics an item must possess, including sufficient detail to show how it is to be manufactured.

Direct Cost: the cost of materials or services identified with only a single cost objective.

Equivalent Items: items that, without actually being identical, have sufficient characteristics in common to be capable of being used for the same purpose.

Encumbrance: the commitment of appropriated funds to purchase an item or service. To encumber funds means to set aside or commit funds for a specified future expenditure.

Evaluation Criteria: those factors specified in the Request for Proposal that will be considered in determining to whom a contract will be awarded.

Full-time Equivalent Position (FTE): the baseline is a full-time position. All part-time positions are converted to the decimal equivalent of a full-time position based on 2,080 hours per year. For example, a part-time typist working 20 hours per week would be the equivalent to .5 of a full-time position.

Fund: an independent fiscal entity with assets; liabilities; reserves; a residual balance, or equity; and revenues and expenditures for undertaking activities.

Generally Accepted Accounting Principles (GAAP): uniform minimum standards for financial accounting and recording, encompassing the conventions, rules, and procedures that define accepted accounting principles.

Goal: a long-term, attainable target for an organization and its vision of the future.

Indirect Cost: an incurred cost that is identified with more than one final cost objective and not specifically associated with any single cost objective.

Interprogram Efficiency: ranks competing programs and allocates the resources to the program that produces the greatest net benefits.

Intersector Efficiency: questions whether or not the spending benefit of government activity yields more benefits to society than if it remained in the private sector.

Intraprogram Efficiency: within each program should combine the resources to maximize the net benefits from any given expenditure increment.

Life Cycle Costing: the total cost of ownership; the total cost of acquiring, operating, maintaining, supporting, and (if applicable) disposing of an item.

Market: the aggregate forces that determine the availability, price, quality, and quantity sold of a specific service or commodity; to perform all activities associated with selling a product or service, such as advertising, packaging, determining need, and identifying and contacting potential purchasers.

Market Segmentation: the process associated with separating various markets into groups for the purpose of identifying risk factors associated with certain commodity/service codes.

Monopoly: a situation where there is one seller and many buyers of a product that has no close substitute and where the seller has considerable control over price because of the lack of competition; the exclusive right to carry on a particular activity.

Objective: a specific, measurable, and observable result of an organization's activity, which advances the organization toward its goal.

Oligarchy: a market situation in which a few companies control or dominate the market for a product or service.

Operating Budgets: all the revenues and expenditures to cover the current fiscal period of the government.

Pareto Principle: a virtual tautology to the effect that "society" was better off if at least some of its members were made better off and no one was made worse off; the principle that states that approximately 80 percent of an organization's time is consumed by 20 percent of the work.

Performance Measures: tools used to measure performance and quantitatively evaluate progress toward planned targets.

Performance Specification: a specification setting forth the capabilities and performance characteristics the article must satisfy.

Policy: a plan, course or action, or guiding principle designed to set parameters for decisions and actions. For a complete definition, please refer to the NIGP *Dictionary of Purchasing Terms*, March 1998, 5th edition.

Pre-bid/Pre-proposal Conference: meeting held with prospective bidders or offerors prior to solicitation of bids/proposals to clarify any ambiguities, answer questions, and ensure all bidders have a common basis of understanding.

Price: the total amount, in money or other consideration, to be paid or charged for a commodity or service; normally includes all costs (direct labor, overhead, materials) and profit or fee.

Price Analysis: the process of examining and evaluating price data without evaluating the separate cost elements or proposed profit to assist in arriving at prices to be paid and costs to be reimbursed.

Procurement Forecast: to tell in advance what probably will happen currently.

Procurement Performance: documentation of the procurement's ability to reach identified benchmarks; procurement's promises and reliability, together with consistency of quality associated with the procurement process.

Procurement Profile: a list of all vendors, sorted by commodity/service code that lists what the organization has spent its resources on.

Profit: the difference between the costs incurred by the contractor to provide the supplies, services, or construction and the amount received from the purchaser in payment.

Qualified Products List (QPL): an approved list of supplies, services, or construction items, described by model or catalogue numbers, which, prior to competitive solicitation, the jurisdiction has determined will meet the applicable specification requirements.

Requirements Analysis: value analysis applied to the writing of specifications to eliminate products or services that are not cost effective.

Restrictive Specification: a specification that unnecessarily limits competition by eliminating items capable of satisfactorily meeting actual needs, often by requiring features which exceed the minimum acceptable characteristics required for satisfactory performance.

Risk Management: the process of planning, organizing, directing, and controlling the resources and activities of an organization in order to minimize the adverse effects of accidental losses at the least possible cost. For a complete definition, please refer to the NIGP *Dictionary of Purchasing Terms*, March 1998, 5th edition.

Sample: one or more units selected from the material or process lot and represented as a specimen of quality.

Specification: a description of the physical or functional characteristics, or the nature of a supply, service, or construction item; the requirements to be satisfied by a product, material, or process indicating, if appropriate, the procedures to determine whether the requirements are satisfied.

Standard: the result of an effort to produce standard specifications; a set of characteristics for an item, generally accepted by the manufacturers and users of the item, as required characteristics for all such items.

Standards Committee: a committee whose purpose is to advise and assist the central purchasing authority in establishing standards and, in some cases, specifications.

Standard Specification: a specification that is to be used for all or most purchases of an item; describes all required physical and functional characteristics of a good, service, or construction.

Standardization of Specifications: the process of establishing a single specification for an item or range of items.

Supply Positioning: a procurement management tool that plots goods and services according to their *relative expenditure* and *difficulty in securing supplies*; a good way to determine where the procurement effort should be focused and where energy and resources should be directed.

Supply Risk: the degree to which the goods and services present risks or are critical to the department/agency, as well as the extent to which a competitive supply market for the goods and services exists.

Tracking and Monitoring Systems: systems to report the progress of implementing the plan and achieving desired results, as demonstrated by specific performance measures.

Vendor File: the accumulated record maintained by the central procurement authority on a vendor, including information on the vendor's relationship with the procurement authority, application for inclusion on the bidders list, record of performance under contract, and correspondence.